MY TRAIN
TO FREEDOM

IVAN A. BACKER

MY TRAIN
TO FREEDOM

A JEWISH BOY'S JOURNEY
FROM NAZI EUROPE TO A LIFE
OF ACTIVISM

*For Lynne,
in friendship

Ivan*

Skyhorse Publishing

Skyhorse Publishing books may be purchased in bulk at special discounts for sales promotion, corporate gifts, fund-raising, or educational purposes. Special editions can also be created to specifications. For details, contact the Special Sales Department, Skyhorse Publishing, 307 West 36th Street, 11th Floor, New York, NY 10018 or info@skyhorsepublishing.com.

Skyhorse® and Skyhorse Publishing® are registered trademarks of Skyhorse Publishing, Inc.®, a Delaware corporation.

Visit our website at www.skyhorsepublishing.com.

10 9 8 7 6 5 4 3 2 1

Library of Congress Cataloging-in-Publication Data is available on file.

Cover design by Brian Peterson

ISBN: 978-1-63450-604-5
Ebook ISBN: 978-1-63450-975-6
Printed in the United States of America

"Activism is my rent for living on the planet."
—Alice Walker

For Nicholas Winton
without whom I would not be alive

For Paula
without whom this memoir would not have been written

TABLE OF CONTENTS

———◆———

PROLOGUE

◆

S IR NICHOLAS WINTON saved my life in 1939, but I didn't know it until
much later.

Winton was a young London stockbroker in 1938 when a friend
invited him to Prague to see the aftermath of the German takeover of
Czech borderlands. Winton realized that Hitler's ambitions would soon
engulf Czechoslovakia and that many people, including children, were
likely to perish. He responded to the Nazi threat by organizing a massive relief effort utilizing trains and boats to save young lives. Winton's
Kindertransports successfully whisked 669 children away from impend-
ing danger. I was one of the children he rescued.

More than sixty years elapsed before I became aware of my savior.
Today, Winton is known as "Britain's Schindler." An award-winning
2011 documentary about his life, *Nicky's Family*, has been distributed
internationally. In 2014, *60 Minutes* aired a report about Winton's life
that featured several clips from the documentary.

Although I did not know many of the details about my escape
until recently, I always knew it was my immense good fortune that I
was saved. I was no more deserving than others. At all times I carry
with me the reminder that I am very lucky to have been spared from
Holocaust brutality.

This memoir recounts how my survival influenced the course of
my life.

PREFACE

———◆———

I HAVE BEEN called upon frequently these past few years to share my story as a Kindertransport escapee from the Holocaust. Suggestions were made that I should record my recollections in a memoir. I put the idea on the back burner until fairly recently when I noticed that my generation is now often referred to as "elders"—a step in aging beyond "senior citizens," which I had become used to hearing. I realized that preserving what those of us who were a part of that history have to say has become an urgent priority.

The blue folder I always take with me when I tell my story to an audience is something of a security blanket. It sits on my side table ready for me to grab on my way out the door. I check that it contains the typed notes I won't consult but always bring along. I will start my talk with a description of my happy boyhood in Prague, then turn to what I remember about my escape in 1939 as a ten-year-old boy aboard a Kindertransport train. Included in the folder is a copy of my poem titled "Trains," which I have been reading aloud at the end of my several talks this past year. Underneath the master copy are several extras in case someone asks for a copy of the poem, which occasionally happens. The DVD of *Nicky's Family*, a documentary about the great humanitarian Nicholas Winton, who organized Kindertransport trains from Prague, has already been delivered to the group sponsoring my presentation and will be screened for the audience prior to my introduction.

As I walk through my foyer to leave by the front door, I pass the large framed poster presented to me in 2012 by the West Hartford Jewish Community Center, where I gave one of my earliest talks to one of the largest and most appreciative audiences. Moving through my condo into that space each day, I often glance at the oversized photograph in the frame—a round-faced gentleman with white hair and a slight twinkle in his eye. The picture is of Nicholas Winton: rescuer of 669 doomed Czech children, including me, who would otherwise have been caught in Holocaust terror. As an escapee I am eternally grateful to this man who saved my life.

In the last few years, I have begun to write vignettes about my boyhood before and after I arrived by train, then boat, in England from Prague as a refugee. I looked back at decisions I made as a young man seeking to establish a life in a new country, America. The fate I had been spared as a child is always with me, and I ponder my worthiness; why was I saved? My thoughts and reflections as an older adult started to knit together and, in combination with my early notes and vignettes, formed a cohesive story—my story. Over the years, I've been in contact with just a few others who had also been on those Kindertransports from Prague, but neither they nor others who'd made the journey had, as far as I could find, published any personal accounts of living in America. I undertook the task of writing this book to document my memories and also to add another voice in admiration of the courageous moral stance taken by Nicholas Winton, who, working with only a few other volunteers, including his mother, Barbara, managed in the short window of time he had to transport so many of us children from Czechoslovakia to safety.

Nicholas Winton's story overarches my own. He accomplished the Kindertransport rescue operation selflessly and with a humbleness that is not found today, a time when the slightest accomplishment is considered newsworthy. The last of Winton's Kindertransport trains did not leave Prague as scheduled in September 1939 because the occupying Nazis closed the Czech borders; the children on that train presumably perished, as did most Jews in Czechoslovakia. After Winton married, he didn't tell his wife about saving Czech children during the war. She accidentally discovered a scrapbook in their attic in 1987—almost fifty years after the event—that documented his wartime work with children, families, adoptive homes in England, and governments. She shared her finding with a television producer who publicized the details on a TV program.

The most dramatic moment in the program came after Winton was identified from the stage and recognized for his life-saving Kindertransports that brought Czech children to safety in 1939. On cue, everyone who had ridden as a child on one of Winton's trains to freedom stood up. Taken by surprise, Nicholas Winton turned around to the silent crowd behind him. Like most in the studio that night, his eyes welled up with tears, and he took out a handkerchief to prevent them from rolling down his cheeks. Unfortunately, I was not present because the organizers of the event did not know how to get in touch with me. I heard that most in attendance lived in England.

I did not know who saved me or the full Kindertransport story until fifteen years later. When I learned of Nicholas Winton and his role in saving my life, I was dumbfounded. I started to read accounts and tried to recall as much as possible about those critical years in which war was beginning.

The Kindertransports from Czechoslovakia were not the first to be organized. Already in the mid-1930s trains and ships were leaving Germany with Jewish children from orphanages and some whose parents were interred in concentration camps. After Kristallnacht in November 1938, there were Kindertransports that took children from Austria and Germany.

The numbers of rescued children swelled. All told, approximately ten thousand children were taken to safety in Great Britain. Only Britain was willing to accept these refugee children—every other country closed its borders to them. The people of the British Isles showed their generosity in taking in so many. Several agencies in England, including Jewish, Quaker, and Christian ones, organized trains, but the plight of Czech and Slovak children was ignored until the German occupation of the Czech Sudetenland, where twenty-nine-year-old Nicholas Winton saw the refugee camps and recognized the situation as dire. No agency was attending to children in Czechoslovakia.

Winton acted on the need to fill this vacuum. He shuttled between his London home and Prague, identifying and recruiting English families willing to sponsor a child, pairing them with eligible children in Prague, arranging for the children's departure, and organizing Kindertransports. Eight Kindertransports were successful. Most of the children said good-bye to their parents before boarding the trains, never to see them again. In this sense my story is different because my immediate family of four escaped. I tell about them and others in this memoir. After Nicholas Winton's story was revealed, he was knighted by Queen Elizabeth II to become Sir Nicholas. The government of the Czech Republic also honored Winton on his several visits to Prague. His "family" has greatly multiplied from the original 669, and he acknowledged all of us as his "children."

I also pay tribute here to my parents and all parents of Kindertransport children for having had the courage and foresight to part with their children—to bestow on them the gift of life, even sometimes at the price of their own lives. Looking at my children and grandchildren when they were at the young ages of those on the Kindertransports, I wonder if I would have been able to do the same. I, too, must have seemed to my parents to be young, dependent, and vulnerable. Yet it is remarkable how many of us children considered the journey an adventure and how trusting we were of our own safety. I acquired the sense that "things will work out in the end," and it has stayed with me throughout my life.

In this memoir I recount ways I have shaped my life in response to these events of my past. For those of us rescued by Nicholas Winton, the task is how to repay our debt for the gift of our lives. Up until his death, Winton revealed his sensitivity to the plight of those in need. Perhaps the legacy of Nicholas Winton will commit us to care more for others.

Finally, I do not refer to myself as a survivor because I did not suffer like others who were unable to leave during the long, murderous Nazi reign. I had no narrow escapes from the Gestapo, no long suffocating rides in trucks and cattle cars, no internment in concentration camps, no brutal forced labor, long inhumane marches, or physical suffering. Unfortunately, this was not the case for many family members and friends. But I lived safely exiled in free countries under circumstances that were initially unfamiliar, but comfortable enough. I escaped.

An intent in writing my story is to investigate the focus—the central question that hangs over my postwar life: *How did the fact that I avoided the Holocaust horrors influence the choosing of my life's work and the major decisions I made along the way?*

This book is a look back at my life but does not try to capture the voice of who I was when the events occurred. It begins in 1939 with Nazi troops marching into Prague, the city of my birth, and my mother's success in obtaining passage for me at age ten to leave on a Kindertransport train for England, where I was placed with several different English families. I detail the adjustments required there of the "Czech boy" and eventually in America where my family and I obtained citizenship. My narrative progresses chronologically and follows my schooling and careers as I wrestle throughout my life to define and act upon the meaning of my survival.

Chapter One: The Kindertransport Kid, 1939

—————◆—————

IT WAS MAY 11, 1939. The dank, dimly lit train platform was crowded that evening at the Masaryk Station in Prague, Czechoslovakia. Masaryk, the chosen name for the busy railroad hub, was in honor of our republic's first president and showed a source of pride nurtured in happier times; the invading Nazis had not yet renamed the streets and places around the city. The station was swarming with German soldiers looking very stern and frightening to me. But what is etched most in my memory is the sixty of us children standing about with numbered tags—my number was 1174—hanging from our necks surrounded by parents, grandparents, and other relatives who had come to see us off on the fourth scheduled Kindertransport from Prague to England. Adults were crying, and hugging and kissing us, fearing they would never see their children again. Some children, particularly the older ones, were trying to wiggle out of the embraces that held them too tightly. Both young and old found it difficult to say good-bye.

The descending dusk further darkened a gloomy sky and mirrored the mood of somber family groups who stood peering down the tracks for the train. With one small suitcase apiece, we young ones were directed to board the Kindertransport that was to take us to safety. Each compartment door opened directly onto the platform, which made it easy for some anguished parents to take their children off the train and then change their minds and suddenly thrust the children back on. Choking

1

back sobs, loved ones fluttered handkerchiefs, dampened with tears, at the train as it pulled away promptly at five o'clock and faded from view.

My mother and aunt were there to see me off, but our farewells lacked the visible emotion of so many around us. My mother was stoic, as she had accepted weeks ago that sending me to England was assuring my survival. I myself was looking forward with excitement to the trip as I had been told my father would be waiting for me at my final destination in London, which was a great comfort since most children had to leave both parents behind. My departure, however, was not as smooth as it appeared to me at the station; I learned later that my leaving was quite difficult for my mother. Not only was she parting with her ten-year-old son, perhaps never to see him again, but she had to endure the rebukes of her sister-in-law, my aunt Malva, who upbraided her vehemently—"You're out of your mind sending the boy off. Do you realize what you are doing? It's terrible!" This incident illustrates the two different points of view among Jews in Prague about the threat posed by Hitler after Czechoslovakia was occupied. Some were certain we must leave the country as soon as possible by whatever means possible, but others thought it would blow over, cautioned calm, said things won't be so bad, believed life as it was for us at the time would endure. Though Mother, too, must have felt some conflict and had certainly worried, she was resolute and would not be deterred. She had become convinced that she was saving me from almost certain death—the tragic fate that befell Malva's two children, both much older than I was.

Our train went north, heading for the German border some seventy-five miles away. I was off on an adventure, unaware of the Holocaust to come. At the border the train stopped for passport checks, but nothing untoward occurred that I remember. Once the Nazi officials saw that our passports had the official Gestapo exit stamp, we were allowed to proceed. I sat next to one of the three adults accompanying our Kindertransport, a lady named Eugenia Tausiková. She was a social worker whom my mother knew, and I was in her care. We occupied a third-class compartment that seated about eight members of our group.

Later that evening we ate the sandwiches brought from home and whatever other goodies were packed with them as the train rolled through Germany. I remember thinking to myself, *I am now in the heart of my mortal enemy's territory, ruled by the hated Nazis,* and I felt some trepidation, but not sustained fear. Above all I felt lonely and could not fall asleep, even while nestled safely on the shoulder of Miss Tausiková. The incessant clickety-clack of train wheels pounded in my head.

I began to think of Father waiting for me at the end of my journey. It had been two months since I last saw him. Father seldom showed outward affection toward me, but he responded warmly and encouraged me whenever I shared my dreams about visiting America, where I imagined I owned a factory managed by my employee, a Mr. Kapusta (cabbage in Czech). I forget what my company manufactured, but there were always problems that Mr. Kapusta invariably solved for me. I looked forward to seeing Father to tell him more of my boyhood fantasies and observing once again the pleasure on his face as he listened to me with complete attention.

Then my thoughts turned to my mother, whom I had left just a few hours before. I kept asking myself when I would see her again. She had promised me she would come to England, too. Mother was not the cuddly type either, but I loved her deeply. She called the shots in our family even though I disliked some of the outcomes, like having to practice the piano, which I considered torture. But I followed through with things I didn't want to do because she insisted. It was she who made the arrangements for my wonderful trips to Dobruška to see my grandparents even when she could not go with me. So many memories of my parents came flooding back on the train.

There was also Frank, eight years older and my only sibling. I hoped I would see him, too, when I reached England. In Prague, Frank and I pursued our own activities, he in secondary school and I in fourth grade. We had different friends because of our age gap, but now I hoped we might establish a closer relationship. I had tremendous respect for Frank because I knew he was smart and he seemed to me to be very independent. I wondered how he was getting along in college, how many new friends he had made and if he missed me. What was he doing this very minute, I mused. I flipped back and forth with thoughts of my separated family members until this mental volleyball rally finally resolved into sleep.

It was morning when the train entered Holland, and I was overwhelmed by a deep sense of relief. I was beyond the reach of Nazis now. We children left the train to have breakfast at the station, served by very friendly Dutch women chattering in an odd-sounding language. Then the journey resumed and continued all day on the same train until we reached Flushing on the English Channel just as evening was closing in. My eyes opened wide when I beheld the large ship that was going to take us across the channel. I had never seen a boat that size, being familiar only with small excursion boats on the Vltava (Moldau) River taking sightseers up- or downstream. I joined an equally excited group of boys, and we roamed the boat from stem to stern, exploring it thoroughly before bedtime. Despite my excitement I was quickly lulled to sleep by the gently rocking surf.

I did not see the east coast of England because we were already docked by the time I awoke. At breakfast I tasted English white bread for the first time and found it revolting. We children agreed among ourselves that it was distastefully spongy, unsubstantial, and almost moist—nothing like the hearty, multi-grain Czech bread we were used to. But we found that when one rolled the white bread into small balls they made very effective missiles—great for shooting at each other. On the last leg of the trip we boarded yet another train to London.

At Liverpool Street Station, all sixty of us were ushered into a large waiting room to meet the sponsoring English families with whom we were to live. My loneliness grew as each name was called that wasn't mine and the number of us left in the hall dwindled. Finally, it came my turn to be introduced to my sponsors, Mr. and Mrs. Miller. I hardly noticed them though because my gaze was fixed on a beaming familiar figure standing slightly behind them—my father. He, too, had been waiting for me.

As I reflect now on my Kindertransport journey and recall experiences that followed in England, I realize how vulnerable and often alone I was, and yet nothing seemed to frighten or faze me very long. There is a resilience in children that enables them to take in stride, as I did, occurrences that might crush adults. Many children across the world face challenging conditions, but they adapt and survive.

Sometimes when I thought about happy times in Czechoslovakia, I felt the grip of homesickness. I tried to comfort myself in those periods of loneliness and isolation by recalling the many pleasant memories I had stored forever from my secure boyhood in the country I loved. My father's arm around me as we walked out of the London train station reassured me.

Chapter Two: Childhood Memories from before the Nazis,
1929–1939

———————◆———————

For a Jewish boy born in 1929 to middle-class parents in Prague, Czechoslovakia, growing up in the 1930s was a comfortable life that seemed full of promise for the future. An unusual feature of my family was that my mother worked outside the home. She gave private lessons in the Czech language to families who spoke mainly German. When Czechoslovakia became an independent country in 1918, Czech became the official language, and those who did not speak it well, or not at all, needed lessons. Since Mother's teaching took place in other people's homes, she was out of the house most days, so a live-in maid was hired who cooked and cleaned for us. My parents, my older brother, and I came home at noon for a substantial lunch together, as was typical of most families those days in our area. After lunch father stretched out on the sofa in the same room for a twenty-minute nap, punctuated by loud snores.

Father was a businessman who managed an iron foundry for the Petzold Company, which produced enameled cast-iron bathtubs. He had a pleasant round face but often wore a sad expression around the family, perhaps because of discomfort from his diabetes, which was not as treatable then as it is today. He loved the game of bridge and would go to his club after work almost daily to play a few hands. He relished telling a good story and was apparently entertaining and skillful at it, yet he rarely revealed his humorous side to me. Music was another of Father's loves. He would anticipate with a low hum the next movement of a composition before it began, much to Mother's annoyance. A major regret of my father's life was that he was not able to take piano lessons when he was young because limited family resources permitted musical instruction only for his older brother, Paul.

My mother was a striking woman with a strong will that stood her in good stead when, later, events turned dangerous. She had a firm chin, aquiline nose, and long hair pulled back into a bun. She has been described as beautiful. Mother knew what she wanted and usually got it one way or another, which did not make her particularly popular with some members of my father's family, especially her brother-in-law, my uncle Paul, who was equally strong-willed.

But Mother's interests did not always coincide with Father's, although both my parents shared a love for music, drama, literature, history, and art. Mother could spend a whole day engrossed in museum exhibits without visibly tiring. She gathered a set of friends of her own and devoted time to them. Languages fascinated Mother and she was fluent in Czech, English, German, and French and could get by in Italian and Spanish; she even spoke a little Russian. Fortunately for my brother and me, these cultural interests of our parents were passed on to us and greatly enriched our lives.

Since my brother, Frank, is eight years older than I, we had little in common. He had his own interests and was busy with his studies. I looked up to him and don't recall ever fighting with Frank. We lived in our own separate worlds, but that changed in later years.

Mother, Father, Frank, and I lived on Veletržní Ulice at number 59, Prague VII, on a busy thoroughfare in a nondescript five-story apartment building with two large units on each floor. We occupied a spacious apartment with five rooms on the top floor, which could be reached either by a slow elevator or by using the stairs. I got great satisfaction running up the stairs, two at a time, and beating my parents who rode the elevator. I would be breathless when I entered our apartment but happy to be the first home. After entering the foyer I walked along a wide, carpeted hall. Opposite the door, a window looked out on a small courtyard lined with white bricks where many pigeons roosted. I liked to stand there observing their view of the world and found the constant cooing soothing. It was part of being home. Slightly to the left of the entrance door was a narrow passage with a pantry on the left side that led to the kitchen from which cooking aromas were inviting to anyone in the immediate area. The smell of Czech soup, which our cook served almost daily, was pungent and always whet my appetite. Arriving home after school, the kitchen was my first stop to drink a glass of milk and feel it trickle all the way down. Milk had to be bought every morning since we had no refrigeration, but it was still adequately chilled in the afternoon.

From the hallway I usually turned left to pass through Mother's bedroom into my room. The dresser in Mother's room fascinated me. It had two wings, each with full-length mirrors, and if I turned them to face each other, I could observe myself in countless images. In the center of my room was a round table draped with an oil-cloth tablecloth where we four family members ate our mid-day meals. Hot soup, often served with dumplings, was a staple, as were hunks of flavorful thick, dark bread, so characteristically Czech.

My toys were kept in a large wardrobe in my room. I loved most to play with my erector set alongside my friend Jirka (George) Bláha, from whom I was practically inseparable. We spent hours constructing huge buildings, the higher and more complicated the better. In another part of the room was the gramophone on which I first heard the Toreador Song from the opera *Carmen*, and I played it often, feeling the beat as I sang along lustily.

There were a few trees in the neighborhood to break up the urban landscape, and at the rear of each building was a little plot of land. I enjoyed this view from my room and frequently surveyed the apartments opposite, straining to see if something was planted in the small gardens that separated the buildings. Although some open spaces were cultivated, others simply afforded a place where people could meet, sit, and talk.

The one bathroom we shared was next to my room, but luckily the toilet had a separate cubicle further down the hallway. Frank would sequester himself there for a prolonged occupation, much to the annoyance of the next person who wanted to use it. That was also true of the bathroom itself, where Father enjoyed luxuriating in prolonged, hot tub baths, taking much time, especially it seemed when Mother was waiting to come in.

I did not frequent the other wing of our apartment often. The library was there with a table for light suppers and snacks and the all-important radio. I distinctly remember a time when I was about eight or nine years old that my parents were huddling near the radio, heads bent while they listened to a rough guttural male voice speaking harshly in German. Although my German vocabulary was inadequate to understand everything he was saying, I knew the shouting frightened my parents and Frank terribly. I observed them shaking their heads in disbelief, but they did not tear themselves away from the broadcast or turn the radio off as I thought they might. I learned that the voice coming through the radio was that of Adolf Hitler telling the world what to expect in the future.

Our formal living room was seldom used except for my hated practice sessions on the stately grand piano placed there. One passed on to the formal dining room, used sparingly for eating, but it contained two beds in opposite corners for Frank and Father since my parents did not sleep in one room together. The smallest room was occupied by our live-in maid. This room had scarcely enough space for her bed and a dresser with an undersized window affording a limited view of the small uninviting courtyard. I wondered how anyone could live in that tiny space, and for me it was strictly off limits so I don't think I was in it more than a couple of times. Many cherished memories of my tranquil childhood are embedded within that apartment I called home for almost ten years.

School was enjoyable and close by—only four blocks away on Vinařská Ulice. I almost finished the fourth grade there. My friend Jirka was from a nearby Catholic family and, as we were in the same class and liked each other, we would often go to his house or mine to play or take walks in Stromovka, a large beautiful park nearby with a path for horses.

Thomas Garrigue Masaryk, the first president of Czechoslovakia, was fond of riding there, and one day we saw him riding all alone. We told everyone who would listen.

• • •

ALTHOUGH WE WERE Jewish we did not observe any traditions or religious observances except that on Yom Kippur my parents would go to temple and I went along once. This religious void was remarkable since my father's boyhood dining room was used as the synagogue in his little town of Kácov and my mother's home in Dobruška was next to the synagogue in which her father took a leading part, but like many European Jews, they had adopted secular practices, and I rarely heard them talk about religion.

I recall living an ideal boyhood during those early years in Prague. As much as music was important to my parents, and I enjoyed listening, too, I never accompanied them to a live concert. Children were not taken to "adult" performances in those days. I reveled in the independence of going about the city alone on the tram or by foot, which even included the walk to my dreaded piano lessons. I took the tram or walked to see my paternal grandmother, who lived quite a long way off. I looked forward to seeing Grandmother regularly every Sunday with other visiting family members and remember that she and my aunt Malva, who lived across the street from her, made wondrous desserts which I enjoyed tremendously.

We had tennis courts close to our apartment, and one day as I was watching the players, one of them noticed me and said, "Would you like to get the balls for us?" What young boy wouldn't be flattered to be asked this? I readily and enthusiastically agreed and spent the whole afternoon running down tennis balls. Unexpectedly, they gave me tips. But I lost track of time and when I got home Mother was furious—"Where have you been? Look at the time!" I thrust out a fistful of coins I thought would surely curb her anger. "Look, I made all this by fetching balls for the tennis players." I was very proud of myself, but she was clearly not impressed. However, this initiated my lifetime love for that sport.

Unfortunately, the tennis court episode was not to be forgotten so easily, as my mother, after contemplating a minute or so, asked me—"So what do you think would be an appropriate punishment?" This surprised and temporarily stumped me. My mind raced to find something that I thought would satisfy her. To this day I cannot fathom how I came up with my suggestion. Had I read about it or heard of some other child having to do it? Suddenly I heard myself saying to my mother, "What if I knelt on some hard dry peas every afternoon for fifteen minutes for a week? Then I could think about what I did." Such a suggestion from her young son must have startled Mother, but after a few grunts she agreed. Dutifully, I found a cardboard box top with low sides and spread out some dry peas from the pantry to set up and prepare to carry out my assigned ordeal, but I had not realized how uncomfortable kneeling on peas would be. It hurt! And contrary to what I told my mother, I did not think about what I had done. I could only count the seconds and minutes until the torture would end.

Vacations in the country were highlights of each year, especially visits to my grandparents, who lived on Shubert Square in Dobruška. For a boy raised in Prague, then a city of a million people, taking a long train ride to a faraway place was not only a welcomed change but a thrilling experience. Trips beyond our city became a routine part of my young life every time I was off from school in summer or winter, and I visited my maternal grandparents. In Dobruška, a small town located in northeastern Bohemia in the foothills of the Orlické Mountains, I formed a warm bond of affection with my beloved maternal grandparents. Because I was not old enough to travel that far alone, when my parents or Frank were not free, a family friend or acquaintance accompanied me. In winter I was met at the railroad station by my grandparents in a sleigh drawn by two horses. I snuggled, all excitement, under a heavy blanket between my grandmother and grandfather as the horses trotted over snow-covered streets to the house. I liked that Grandmother fussed over me and kept checking to make sure I was warm enough.

Many pleasures were in store for me during those winter visits with my family in Dobruška. I still remember the big hill on which town children would assemble with sleds ready to test who could go downhill the fastest and furthest before trekking back up to repeat the ride again. Christmastime was especially thrilling. Not only were there presents, but I saw my first Christmas tree, ablaze with real lit candles at a neighbor's house. It was a mesmerizing sight for young eyes!

Watching my grandparents' three family cats in the snow-covered terrain was like seeing fish flopping about on dry land. The cats would shake their paws violently every two or three steps before taking the plunge off the balcony at the back of the house onto an adjoining snow-covered wall to land gracefully in the street. Since litter boxes were unknown in those days, the felines had to be let out several times a day, a household ritual starting early each morning. One of the male cats was my grandfather's favorite, and every workday morning the cat would jump on Grandfather's shoulder for the daily ride to the office of his textile business located on the ground floor next door. There kitty would settle on top of the stand-up desk and sagely observe the goings-on of workmen, or sleep, as matched his mood. At the end of the day the cat was conveyed back home in the same manner as he arrived I marveled at their relationship.

Although in his eighties when I was a small child, Grandfather still worked each day, especially after his oldest son, my uncle Karel who was in the family business, died prematurely. On weekends of good weather, Grandfather would always take a walk along one of the main roads that in those days were almost devoid of traffic. He walked briskly, so rapidly in fact that I had trouble keeping up on my much shorter legs. Many times we walked as far as the small garden plot of land he owned. In the center stood an enclosed gazebo-like summer house where we could rest and where the family often picnicked on leisurely summer days. Later in life whenever I read accounts of lovers meeting for trysts in summer houses, I visualized the summer house of my grandparents amidst blooming meadow flowers in the garden at Dobruška.

My grandparents' house in town was next door to the synagogue. Whereas he was not a particularly religious man, my grandfather, by reason of his proximity, assumed responsibility for the synagogue's maintenance and made sure things ran smoothly. During services the women, by tradition relegated to the balcony reserved for them, tended to gradually talk louder as their attention wavered from the religious observances below to subjects more directly linked to their daily lives, which they found more compelling to talk about. Grandfather didn't approve of the chatter and would stand, deliberately turn around to the balcony, and issue forth a loud "shhhhhhhh" audible to everybody. That quieted the women, but only temporarily.

While Grandfather spent long hours in the office, my grandmother oversaw the household. I recall her early morning planning sessions with the cook to decide lunch and supper menus. Like my grandfather, my grandmother was a gentle, loving person. Together they created a warm welcoming household that became very lively on holidays when my mother's younger sisters arrived, one from Berlin and the other from Bratislava. Both were vivacious and, to my delight, added spirit to the festivities.

One morning I was awakened by a vigorous tickling all over and I knew my aunt Vala, short for Valerie, had arrived for a visit. She had no mercy and kept on till I was out of bed. My reward was a bear hug, which I gladly reciprocated. She took a special interest in me as a young boy, perhaps because she had no children and was not married, or perhaps because I was the youngest of her nephews. I always had fun with Vala as she took me around my grandparents' little town and told me about the big city where she lived—Berlin, the capital of our enemy.

Other frequent visitors were Mother's youngest sister, Mila, and her husband Boleslav. They had no children either and that again may be a reason they fussed over me so, which, of course, I enjoyed. Mila was a vegetarian and often prepared her own entrees. She would visit a neighboring farm each morning to get goats' milk, which she relished but I decidedly did not like. Boleslav was a Catholic, and aunt Mila converted early in their marriage. Boleslav joined the resistance movement during the war, and he was betrayed, arrested, and sent to the Flossenbürg concentration camp. He wrote a gripping account of the death march he was on from Flossenbürg. I translated his manuscript from Czech and include it here in Appendix 1. Boleslav, and later his family, hid Mila and saved her from the Nazis.

When my grandparents' house was full of guests, I had to sleep in their bedroom on a couch converted to a bed. When Grandmother came into the room after I was in bed and prepared to wash up in the basin full of hot water she carried from the kitchen, she would always first caution me, "Ivánku (a Czech diminutive) turn your head now. I don't want you to be peeking." I never peeked.

Also living in Dobruška was Jenda, my cousin just a couple of years older than me. We played endlessly with his collection of cars while he told me about his friends in school, and sometimes we watched activities from his balcony taking place on the town's main square below. We tried to keep up our friendship by written correspondence between my visits. Jenda was murdered in the Holocaust.

The one source of friction between my grandparents was Grandmother's expensive tastes. When she took the train to Prague to shop, she would always spend too much money according to her husband. She insisted on being well-dressed and chose neckwear that would hide the prominent goiter growing on her neck. To camouflage it she wore lace collars that always had to be clean; the collar was part of her distinctive uniform. When she was shipped off to the Terezín (Theresienstadt) concentration camp in 1942, she wore her lace collar as usual. In the squalid conditions of living in one room with a dozen others, she still managed to wash her collar each day to keep it fresh. It was her quiet way of affirming her dignity and individuality under extreme conditions. Survivors who knew her invariably commented on that act whenever they remembered my grandmother.

Grandmother's adventurous younger brother, Frank, after whom my brother is named, was a favorite of my mother, and he knew of Grandmother's penchant for fine things—including jewelry. On a visit in the early part of the twentieth century after Frank returned from a prolonged stay in America, mostly in Colorado, he waited one evening until the table was cleared after supper then took a small pouch from his pocket. He emptied the contents carefully onto the felt table cover—diamonds, rubies, amethysts, and emeralds tumbled out. He looked at my grandmother and said, "Jenny, choose one!" and with great delight and no hesitation she did. Mother suspected that the precious stones were her uncle Frank's gambling winnings in the "new world."

Often on Monday nights in Dobruška during the summer, I could not easily fall asleep because I was anticipating what I would wake up to the next morning. I was never disappointed. The square below my window was transformed overnight into rows of portable stalls selling everything from vegetables, flowers, and clothing to live animals. The cacophony sounded like a carnival with squealing piglets, quacking ducks, crowing roosters, and cackling hens, and in the background was the steady incessant buzz of people heartily greeting each other and bartering loudly. Only the rabbits in their cages were quiet.

I would dress as fast as I could, and after gulping down some breakfast ran outside to wander from one booth to the next, being careful not to interrupt the buying and selling and the accompanying conversations of involved negotiators. The animals were first on my mind and I petted all that would let me get close. The roosters were the dangerous ones as they would charge my hand, so I made it a game to see if I could withdraw quickly enough to avoid their sharp beaks. The bunnies were my favorites, with soft fur that I stroked gently. I knew why they were there but didn't let myself think about their little lives about to be snuffed out. I spent hours meandering and never ceased to be fascinated by the chatter and commotion that permeated the square on market day.

Grandmother would arrive at the market early to carefully inspect the greens in every stall before finally making a purchase. She would buy fresh eggs, home-baked bread, vegetables, of course, and cheese sometimes if a taste of it met her approval. She had but a short walk to transport her purchases home.

As dusk approached, the square would begin to empty out and I'd be sorry to see another market day draw to a close. Those who sold

out their wares left first, and then one by one each stall was disman-
tled and disappeared. Darkness would settle over the square, and by my
bedtime everything would be as it was the day before, hushed after the
day's excitement, the quiet interrupted only by the prolonged chirping
of crickets. Each Tuesday night I had no trouble going to sleep after the
eventful day. Exhausted but content, I would quickly drop off, eagerly
awaiting the next week's market day. I am thankful that I corresponded
faithfully with Grandmother up until war broke out, when all communication ceased. Life in Dobruška continued until the tragic turn of 1942
when my grandparents along with Jews from other parts of the country
were herded into the Terezín concentration camp.

One embarrassing incident blemishes my otherwise happy childhood interactions with other Czech children. I owned a soccer ball, and
Jirka and I often took the ball to a nearby playground for use in pickup
games. One day when it was not needed, we stuck it under a jacket to
act as a goal post then forgot about it. The ball appeared to be missing
when we gathered our things and prepared to go home. I convinced
myself that a group of older boys playing nearby had taken it. Jirka and
I mustered up the courage to approach them; we walked into the middle
of their game and directly accused them of taking my ball. Ours was a
poorly planned strategy. Annoyed, they stopped their game and brought
their ball over, scratched off the dirt to reveal a bright yellow color, and
then, glaring, shouted at us, "Is your ball yellow?" It was not, and we
hightailed it out of there before they could justify beating us up or at
least making us apologize. This taught me a valuable lesson that I never
forgot: before you accuse someone, make sure you offer proof.

The agreeable times and happy experiences of my boyhood were
interrupted by the 1938 crisis that ended with the Munich Agreement.
As Hitler's threats escalated in late summer, my parents became concerned for our physical safety. No one knew what was going to happen, and as a precaution I was shipped off to friends in the countryside.
After the agreement was signed on September 30, 1938, that ceded
the Sudetenland of Czechoslovakia to Germany, I returned to Prague.
While there was a certain relief that the immediate crisis had passed,

the air was thick with apprehension and questions of whether or not this agreement would stop Hitler or encourage him. The raging debate in the Jewish community was whether to get ready to leave or to stick it out. That question was answered on March 15, 1939, a day of infamy for my country. I was in fourth grade, walking to school several blocks away on a heavily overcast gray day and made my usual stop for Jirka. As we walked toward the main avenue in our neighborhood, we witnessed people shaking their heads and some were crying. What was happening?

But we immediately understood when we saw armored trucks roll by with huge black swastikas displayed followed by motorcycles with sidecars occupied by helmeted soldiers in gray uniforms that mirrored the weeping sky. In school we learned the awful truth that our beloved democratic country had been forcefully and illegally occupied by a behemoth mortal enemy, Germany's Nazi Third Reich. Czechoslovakia was no longer. It fell like a pawn knocked over in a grand international chess game. Having been betrayed by Great Britain, France, and the Soviet Union at Munich, my country was left totally defenseless and now our freedom had vanished.

Without delay Mother began my preparations to leave for the distant shores of England. Two months later I was in a strange land, living with a new family, trying to cope with a language I could not understand, and looking toward a new life that would change me forever.

Chapter Three: The Rest of My Family Escapes, One by One, 1939

———————◆———————

My IMMEDIATE FAMILY was extremely lucky. All four of us—Father, Mother, Frank, and I—were able to escape the clutches of Nazi peril, albeit we fled separately, taking advantage of a relatively brief window in time that was open to us.

My Father, Benno

Father was the first to leave, boarding a five o'clock train from Prague on March 14, 1939. In the early hours of the very next morning, Nazi troops occupied our country. Father's trip was arranged back in January with the Petzold Company that employed him, and he considered himself to be leaving on a regular business trip. Mother, however, viewed this as an opportunity to begin family escapes. Her insight about upcoming danger came through advice she heard, some given directly to her while she was at her tutoring jobs. Father had his ticket for several weeks before he actually left, and at that time one did not need a visa to enter Great Britain, only a valid passport. Mother insisted he take extra clothing with him when the day for his leave-taking was set and he started to pack, but Father remained ambivalent and unsure about making the trip. In fact, he called my mother from Berlin not long after he departed, in distress. "I am coming home. You are there with the children all alone and I need to come back." Years later Mother mimicked for me her vehement response—"Don't you dare!" She said a similar conversation took place from London.

Mother also discovered that, before he left, Father had withdrawn all the money from their bank account in order to repay funds he had borrowed from his very wealthy uncle Emil. She learned later that Father wanted to have a clean financial slate and not owe money to anyone, but he had not disclosed this to her at the time of the withdrawal, and she was furious! It fell to her to ask Emil for the money again. Going to him was painful and humiliating because he did not like Mother. But she was relieved to ultimately receive some of the money back from Emil as she was quite in need of it.

My Brother, Frank

Frank had to get out of Czechoslovakia before April 1. There was still time between March 15, when the Nazis began their occupation of Czechoslovakia, and the end of March, during which a visa was not a requirement to enter Great Britain. But a number of permits had to be obtained for him to make the deadline. Since Frank had already been accepted at Margate College, in England, leaving the country should have been no problem—but it was. The English representative of Margate College in Prague needed to certify that Frank had been accepted and most of the tuition was already paid. Mother tried to call this man to expedite the certification approval, but for a reason nobody could understand, he kept dodging her even though time was running out and international tensions were rising. She finally decided on the following strategy, described in her own words:

> I went to my English teacher, Miss Hands. She was an admirable woman, but old and not well. I said to her, "You have to have the generosity to get up at six o'clock in the morning and accompany me to see this man. I cannot budge him, and I cannot reach him. But at 6:00 a.m. the maid cannot say that he is not in. You are British, and you can talk to him in a way which I could never do."

Miss Hands agreed, and she did it. I can still see her before me. She took a taxi and met me at the door to the man's apartment. It was 6:00 a.m. and we got him out of bed, quite literally. Miss Hands spoke beautifully. She said, "You cannot do this. You have accepted several thousand francs. This boy has to get out. It was promised after all."

I cannot recall the words, of course, but it was an inspiring confrontation—the man in pajamas and Miss Hands in righteous indignation. And he did it. He wrote out the confirmation, there at that moment, that Frank was accepted and that he has to be in England for the beginning of the term."

But there was one more hurdle for Frank—to obtain an exit permit from the Gestapo, which was necessary to leave the country. Because the certification of acceptance to Margate College was now official, the Gestapo eventually stamped Frank's passport, but to accomplish this he had to stand in line for twenty-four hours at the Gestapo office. Mother brought him food so he would not have to give up his place in line. With Frank's departure from Czechoslovakia, half of our family unit was now safe in England.

My Mother, Alice

After I boarded the Kindertransport train in May of 1939, my mother alone remained in Prague, and she had the most difficult escape of us all. Mother described her dangerous and harrowing flight to England in an interview I recorded with her years later. The following is the account in her own words:

I was waiting for a domestic [work] permit. Britain was being flooded with refugees and new rules were put in effect. You had to have proof that you would have a job when you arrived and would not be a public charge. That permit was not forthcoming. Through the owner of the boarding house where he was staying in London, Father was trying to get a permit for me. Finally, I got a letter that I was being hired by a Mrs. Barrett in Berkhamsted, in Hertfordshire, about one and a half hours by train from London. She was going to pay me thirty pounds a year.

I got the work permit at the beginning of August, but by that time, the Germans had made stricter rules about letting Jewish people go. You had to apply at a large office in Dejvice [a section of Prague]. The Jewish community itself ran the office.

You know, all through the Nazi reign, one of the many despicable aspects of their operation against the Jews was that they used the Jewish communities to run the red tape of their own persecution. Here was an early example of it: a Jewish committee made to administer the Nazi laws on Jewish emigration.

But, at that moment, I was too preoccupied with my own problems for general reflections. I had to get to England and a whole new list of rules applied. The Gestapo permit on which Frank had left was no longer available. The Jewish Committee had to issue a permit. They checked that your taxes were all paid, and any number of other details. The permit then went to the Gestapo for a final approval. The Gestapo had an office in the same building.

You had to wait to receive official permission to come to Dejvice. It was forbidden to try to speed up the process. I would have liked to go to the committee and explain that my British visa was valid for thirty days, and that it would expire on September 1st. It was forbidden. And I knew that after September 1, I would have to apply anew for the British visa. The process would go back to step one. I might never get out.

On August 31st I went there, knowing it was forbidden, and stood in line outside. The man at the gate was a friend. He looked the other *way while I smuggled myself in. Once inside, I skirted all of the tables of the Jewish Committee and went around to the back to the Gestapo room. There I stood in the corridor in front of an open door, and, of course, I did not go in. What I was doing was forbidden, but an unauthorized entry into a Gestapo office was more forbidden than everything else put together. I waited for hours.*

The Gestapo man in charge was Officer Lederer. He was famous throughout Prague for his power, his ruthlessness, and his good looks. He had seen me standing there without a word. He himself would not say anything. It was a standoff until they wanted to close up. Then he finally said, "What about you standing there all this time?"

And then I spoke up. I poured out my entire story. He reached into a compartment, picked out a document, stamped it, and threw it at me. He knew exactly where it was, and he saved my life. It was the day before Hitler moved into Poland on September 1st.

Of course, I could not know for sure that he would have my passport. But there was a good chance that the Jewish Committee had processed it. It had been there for a month. And that Gestapo office was the next step and the last required. And, indeed, it was there. They had been sitting on my passport.

In the morning of September 1st, I went with my maid to Wilsonovo Nádraží. [This was another railroad station in Prague; it was named for President Woodrow Wilson, who helped found modern Czechoslovakia through the Versailles Peace Treaty in 1918]. *She was very decent and helped me with the luggage. At the station, we were told "no trains, no trains." Hitler had invaded Poland and no passenger trains were running.*

I telephoned Miluška [the wife of Father's younger brother, Leo] *and she saved me at that point. She telephoned the Šmolkas. They were already in England. She knew that Mr. Šmolka's driver had the car (in Prague) and this driver took me to the border beyond Pilsen. Miluška went with me. I had two heavy suitcases and one small one.*

I just left the apartment. I told the maid she could have the dining room set. The apartment was half empty. I had sold the piano. The "lift" [the shipment crate] with the furniture had been packed for the move to England. What was left was the entire kitchen and some couches. There wasn't much there.

The "lift" was also saved thanks to Miluška. The movers could not move it now because of the war. Miluška had it stored in Mr. Šmolka's garage. There it survived the war, in a way. By the time it came to the United States, half of it was gone, robbed. The best pieces were gone. [Two good items survived, a bookcase and a chandelier. See Chapter Fifteen for their interesting fate.]

Mr. Šmolka's chauffeur brought the suitcases to the border, to the gate. He could not go any further. He left them there. Miluška and I were both crying. Then the car turned around and left.

I don't know how to describe it: You know, I was alone, and it was a fantastic adventure just to come to the border. But it was legal. The Germans are very precise. When they see a passport which is validly stamped, they will not say, "You Jewess, we will not let you into Germany." That was the irony—it was an impossible situation. They, the Germans, carried my suitcases in and somebody said, "There is a train—not a passenger train but a freight train—going to Nuremberg. If you want to go by train to Nuremberg, you can catch it." So I went on that train all through the night to Nuremberg.

In Nuremberg, there was a congress of the Nazi party. You can't imagine what that was like. There were blood red flags from roof to pavement on every street. It was frightening.

I had some money legally. And some I wanted to send to Vala [Mother's youngest sister in Berlin]. This part I had hidden. When I arrived at the station in Nuremberg, I was told there were no trains. I had wanted to go to Aachen and to the Belgian border at Aix. They told me, "If you have money, you can hire a taxi and there will be a train in Cologne." I hired a taxi for 150 marks, which was half the money I had. I found a taxi driver who was willing to take me to Cologne, but he wanted to see the money first. He said, "If you show me the money, I will take you." I showed it to him and he took me.

That is a trip I will never forget. It was very far. And it was the loveliest weather imaginable. Germany is such a lovely country. But the contrast of being desperate, half out of my mind—I did not know if I would ever arrive in England—this contrast of going by car like a tourist, the lovely weather, and the countryside, and being in such distress…

It was the afternoon of September 2nd. Every train was going to Poland, so very few trains were left. But in Cologne there was a train going west. I bought a ticket with the remaining "legal" money I had.

On the train there was a group of hysterical German women who said, "You will never get to Belgium via Aachen. You should go through the enclave"—that was a German protectorate area. I don't know why I listened to them, but I did. It was probably a bad idea. I got off the train at the stop they indicated.

It was the middle of the night, a small station on the German side of the Belgian border. There was one soldier, one nurse, and one official, the commandant. I told them I had no money, no contraband, or anything. The nurse appeared and made me strip. Of course, she found the money that I had wanted to send to Vala.

Now, they woke up the commandant. He came down, and he shouted and carried on, "You shut up. You know that I can have you arrested and jailed, you Jewess, you dirty Jewess." Then they opened up the suitcases and just emptied them. Everything was out on the floor. He took my money. Then I had not one cent left. But he did not take anything from the suitcases. He just took every bit of money. But I did have a visa and a valid passport, so if he didn't arrest me for trying to smuggle out the money, he would have no reason for stopping me. And since he took all the money, he took pity on me and let me go.

It was 2:00 a.m. After I repacked the suitcases, I went out of the station. It was pitch black. I asked the only soldier there, "Where is the Belgian border?" He pointed to a red light and said, "There is Belgium."

I went three times, carrying one suitcase at a time. Each trip took half an hour. My purse also must have weighed about twenty kilos. The Belgian sentry looked at me as if I were a ghost, but the border guards spoke French and they took me in without money. They even bought me coffee. There was a train to Brussels at 6:00 a.m. and they put me on it. On the train I told the conductor that I had no money and he let me go on through to Brussels. That I will never forget. It isn't very far. Belgium is a small country. It was about a two hour ride, but still...

In Brussels, I was safe. There was Mr. Aaron, a friend of Father's, and he lent me money. I also had a former student there, Mr. Volner, who had a gift shop, and he also lent me money. I also had a French visa and I thought I would go and see the countess—a very close longtime friend, La Countess de Colorado—but Mr. Aaron said, "You must be crazy. This is not a pleasure trip. How do you know you will ever get out of France? This is war. You go nicely to England." He was right.

But during her journey Mother made a one-day detour anyway, as she had heard about a special exhibit of paintings by Peter Paul Rubens in Antwerp and she was determined to see it. She took an early train and arrived on the gallery steps only to find it was closed. Undeterred, Mother rang the bell. Rang it again, and again, and again, until finally the museum director himself came to find out who was so insistent. She explained that this was the only day she could be in Antwerp and she desperately desired to view the Rubens exhibit. Her pleas won him over and he let Mother in. All day, quite alone and unguarded, she drank in the magnificence of Rubens's huge canvasses until she returned late to Brussels, exhausted but soon ready to resume the final challenges to reach family and freedom.

I stayed another night in Brussels, and the next day I took a ship from Oostende to England. I arrived on September 4th, one day after war was declared.

In England, I went to work for Mrs. Barrett, the woman who had pledged to employ me. She was a shrewd old hag, a ninety-two-year-old miser who lived with her insane daughter. When I arrived, she dismissed all her servants and planned to get full value for the thirty pounds she had pledged to pay me for a year.

But I soon found good employment as a governess to a wealthy family, the Dunns. Despite the loud squawks of protest from Mrs. Barrett, I left to work for the Dunns who invited me to bring you [Ivan] to live with me in their house.

In six months the four of us had effectively escaped the Nazis and were counted among the saved but, like others, scars remained into our futures. My childhood was irrevocably interrupted in 1939 by the German invaders who initiated a merciless reign of terror on relatives left behind and on my country. That year, after arriving on the Kindertransport, I was fortunate to be relocated in a free nation to resume boyhood with three different English families, each one providing me a unique experience.

Chapter Four: My Three English Families, 1939

———————◆———————

To conform with British Home Office regulations, each Kinder-transport child needed a British sponsor to live with, and I was placed with the Millers who became my first family in the new country. Although my father was already in London, I could not live with him because he had only one small furnished room in a rooming house.

The connection with the Millers was made through my brother, Frank. He and Cyril Miller, the family's eldest son, became friends when they both stayed the month of August 1938 in Saint-Malo, Brittany, with a French family to learn French. Frank wrote to Cyril asking if his parents would sponsor me—and they did. The placement must have made it easier for Nicholas Winton to include me on one of his Kindertransports since he did not have to locate a sponsoring family as I already had one. Each British family accepting a child had to put up fifty pounds, a significant sum of money in those days. Winton searched tirelessly for families, but almost two thousand children remained on his list of names needing sponsors, and those children did not escape the Nazi war machine that swallowed up Czechoslovakia.

The Millers seemed to me to be a strange family. Mr. Miller was a businessman who made a substantial sum of money which he liked to draw attention to whenever possible. He was especially proud to own one of the first television sets. It had only about a ten-inch screen but was big enough to view a Joe Louis boxing match with a group of friends invited over for the occasion. I watched, too, much to the amazement and chagrin of my schoolmates who did not have TVs and had to endure my enthusiastic descriptions of the progression of the fight.

While Mr. Miller was a short stout man in his forties or fifties, his wife was tall with dark hair and penetrating eyes; she was very high strung. Her adored pet was a little poodle-like dog, and it appeared to me she devoted more time to her dog than to her two teenage sons, Cyril and Harold. Both boys were at school, away more than they were home. The Millers lived very comfortably in a single-family house within middle-class surroundings of north London; a well maintained park was situated nearby. Theirs was a quiet neighborhood consisting of similar type houses built about the same time. One evening a mysterious puddle appeared on the Millers' staircase landing. There was no doubt in my mind how it got there, but at first Mrs. Miller was perplexed by the discovery. She stared down at the dampness then looked directly at me with squinted eyes. "Why couldn't you wait to get to the bathroom? What's wrong with you!" she admonished me with disgust. "*But I didn't do it!*" I protested, and then added, "The dog must have done it." But she would hear none of this theory, dismissed it at once, and made clear to me that her precious pet would never do that in her nice home. She finished her rant with, "You should be quite ashamed of yourself!" I can still see her red face staring down into my pale one.

I looked forward to seeing Father every Sunday afternoon. He visited me without fail and always brought sweets with him to nibble on while we walked in the park, sat on one of the benches, and talked. It was a pleasure to converse in Czech again, to hear news about the rest of the family, especially about my mother, who was still stuck in Prague. We spoke not only about the family but also about what was occurring in Europe, the likelihood of war engulfing our country, and together we speculated about strategies. In fact, over time the progress of the war became the main topic of our conversations. My father was not a very demonstrative man, seldom revealing what was on his mind or his feelings, but I absorbed great warmth just being with him at those times.

Going to synagogue on the Sabbath was another new experience. Our family was secular Jews—my parents seldom went to temple. But with the Millers I was required to attend services regularly and found it a strange experience, mysterious and alien.

Come summer, it was time for a vacation at the "seaside," and in the Miller's case this was at Ramsgate in Kent. Even though war clouds were hovering ominously over Europe, I spent several pleasurable weeks playing there with other London children "on holiday." When we were driving to Ramsgate with mister at the wheel, his wife beside him, and me in the back seat enjoying the ride, the missus suddenly let out a blood-curdling shriek that made me hold my breath, thinking we were about to experience a major crack up. Instead, with little break in speed, Mr. Miller was squeezing the car between a trolley and a truck, accomplishing the tight maneuver without a scratch. After skillfully making it through, Mr. Miller looked over at his wife's frightened face and roared with laughter.

On the Monday after my arrival in May, I was taken to the neighborhood elementary school and put into the third grade. Although my mother had taught me some English in Prague, I could communicate very little and understood less. My one moment of glory came on the school playground one day in a game resembling cricket or stickball. I caught a very high fly ball which everyone expected me to drop. I was just as surprised as they to see the ball resting securely in my bare hands; but I quickly decided not to reveal how ecstatic, and surprised, I was, instead assuming an off-hand attitude of casual confidence as I trotted off the field with my team.

When classes resumed at the end of the summer, Germany had just invaded Poland and England declared war. One day during the first week of school, we were told to come the following day with a suitcase containing just our basic belongings and be prepared to leave. All London children were being evacuated to the midlands in anticipation of bombing attacks on the city. So, I was on the move again, and it was good-bye to the Millers for good.

We children arrived by train in Northampton, were divided into groups at the station, and marched into a residential area. At each intersection, ten of us were dispatched with a lady who knocked at every front door of each two-story row house occupied by a working class family. The lady asked a standard question after the woman of the house opened her door. "These are children from London—how many can you take?" What a contrast with the London neighborhood of my first placement! These were families getting by on the husband's meager salary while the wife kept house and tended to a brood of children. There were no television sets here.

There were only two of us left when the end of the dead-end street came into view. I began to panic, worried about what would happen if none of the three remaining houses had room for us or, worse, if I alone was not chosen. But at the third house from the end, the woman answering the door said cheerfully, "Well, I have a son at home and he has a double bed all to himself. We can fit these two in there. I'll take them both." That night I learned to sleep with two companions wedged in beside me! But I was happy I had a bed to sleep in and dozed off quickly. In a few weeks the other boy from London moved out to a different family and I had the luxury of half a bed. But we were not the only ones to have to share. In the next bedroom were two daughters sleeping in a double bed with their aunt.

At the end of the street was a retaining wall beyond which stretched a wide expanse of open meadowland with a stream meandering lazily through it. As I was to find out, the stream flooded after heavy rains but the retaining wall kept us dry. I loved to roam the fields and even tried my hand for the first time at fishing—not successfully.

One sunny afternoon, three of us boys wandered a bit further beyond the wall than usual and discovered a brick building with rail tracks leading to it. When we looked through the grimy window, we saw a large shiny black locomotive. We were inside in a jiffy. Once on the platform of the engine, our imaginations took off—down the tracks and through the meadow the locomotive carried us, clickity-clacking rhythmically and tooting its whistle until dusk came when we suddenly realized we had better return with haste back to reality.

Northampton lasted for me a little more than two months. The family there, whose name I cannot recall, was very kind to me and shared their home without complaint even though they lived quite modestly. Saturday evening baths were memorable. The missus would heat up water on the stove, pour it into a portable metal half-bath in the middle of the kitchen and then wash each one of us separately. "Are you clean?" I would nod. "Well, wrap yourself in a towel and off with you. NEXT!" she bellowed. After a week of washing only hands and face, the bath felt so good that I was pokey about getting out. I learned that modesty is not possible in such close quarters; and it was there, on the living room floor, with the two daughters, that I timidly received my first basic sex education lesson.

Friends of the family who visited would ask me, "How did you get here and when did you leave Prague?" Expressing incredulity and exuding sympathy they added, "You say you haven't seen your mother for six whole months?" That was my cue to tell my story in a hushed voice with a sad face and sometimes tears as well. I was fairly shameless about it and discovered that more tears produced more kisses and cuddling. I enjoyed the attention and did not feel guilty about playing on the emotions of my listeners. All in all, I was not unhappy living with this second English family in Northampton.

By November I was reunited with my mother and able to go live with her. She had arrived in England the day after war broke out, following a harrowing journey filled with danger. She was hired as governess and tutor for the children of a well-to-do family, the Dunns, in Bromham, Wiltshire, a small village between Chippenham and Devizes. Major and Mrs. Dunn had agreed to let me come live there with my mother in their large home called Battle House.

Horses and hounds first welcomed me when I arrived at Battle House, the Dunn's estate, from Northampton as a ten-year-old on that memorable November morning before the jaws of war clamped firmly around Great Britain. A fox hunt was about to begin. With all the excitement, it was a while before I located my mother, whom I last saw on the railroad platform in Prague before I boarded the Kindertransport train, now more than six months ago. When at last I saw her hurrying toward me, I tingled with anticipation. I noticed at once that Mother wore a big bandage on one of her fingers, covering a painfully infected wound. Later, I was relieved to learn the injury was recent—the result of an exploding hair dryer, not due to any occurrence on her perilous journey to England.

Major Dunn, patriarch of Battle House, was in the British army and served long hours at the military base. The major, who cut an imposing figure especially in his army uniform, had a ruddy complexion and a neatly trimmed mustache. I saw at once that he ruled the roost when he was home, and, as he was stationed nearby, he was home most weekends. The major always stood or sat ramrod straight as befitted his military rank and family position, and most children and adults at Battle House stayed clear of him. The children, me included, usually ate in our own room, which served as the schoolroom, nursery, and playroom, as well as our dining room, but on Sundays we had dinner with the grown-ups around the sturdy long oak table in the formal dining room. Children did not speak unless spoken to, and we were always on our best behavior at those times. During one Sunday dinner I remember well, I jumped in alarm when Major Dunn raised his deep bass voice to boom out at one of his sons—"Hugh, stop waving your fork all around the countryside!" I had never heard a human voice with such volume. I still recall these tense dinners at the Dunns' table, and specifically this episode, when I read novels or see dramas about the English upper class.

Mrs. Dunn, the strong-willed mistress of Battle House, was a short, intense woman who liked to drink and smoke pungent Turkish ciga-rettes. Once I filched one of her cigarettes and lit up while sitting on a back wall. In short order I became thoroughly dizzy and fell hard off my perch to the ground. I permanently foreswore smoking then and there, which wasn't a bad thing.

There were many Dunn children around for companionship. Mrs. Dunn had been married previously to a Mr. Austin and had three children from that marriage, all now in their mid-teens—Basil, Joy, and

Bill. At their holiday visits it was a full house when they joined the three Dunn children, Pierre, Hugh, and Minette—all slightly younger than me. With Bill, who was a couple of years older, I explored the attic and roof parapets of the large and impressive country house. Joy Austin, sixteen, was lovely, and I promptly, and privately, fell in love with her. Basil, the oldest, asked me to pump air for the organ in the village church next to Battle House, and I was enchanted with its sound. I appreciated the instrument even more years later after I married my wife, a trained musician who concentrated her music studies on the organ and became a church organist. A seventh child was added to the Dunn household a year later when Petronelle was born. Mother helped take care of her and I was fascinated to watch the baby being bathed and diapered since I had never seen a newborn close up and knew nothing about their care.

Although Battle House could boast no hunting dogs, there were three dogs in residence. Rounding out the household was Simba, a lion-colored African breed of hound dog with a unique band of hair, about eighteen inches long, that stood straight up on her spine, and she was fiercely devoted to Mrs. Dunn; Susi, a calm, lovable black lab was my favorite; and there was Rory, a mangy old brown cocker spaniel who smelled and was seldom allowed inside. But I gave Rory attention and liked to feed him since he was so grateful and rewarded me with a fast wagging of his tail. There were also servants—Sheila the cook, Beryl the maid, and Mr. Duck, chauffeur, gardener, and groom, whom I was immediately assigned to help. Theirs was an active household.

Since Christmas was coming soon, it was decided that I should not start school until after the holidays. Mr. Duck placed me in charge of the chickens, feeding them and collecting their eggs. But I learned even the most straightforward job has challenges. One day a fox burrowed under the chicken coop, disrupting my newly learned routine and hor-rifying me when I realized several of my chickens became his victims. I was sorry for the chickens and disappointed that I had not seen the fox because I had never seen one. The next day I worked with Mr. Duck to fortify the henhouse against intruders, a formidable task.

Over time I gathered other assignments. The adults at Battle House showed great creativity in devising a variety of jobs and responsibilities for me. In the house it was my duty to tend the coal stove that heated the entire house, and I learned how to correctly bank it for the night so the fire never went out. I was proud to be assigned this responsible task. Before turning in at night I also had to place hot water bottles at the bottom of each bed in the house since bedrooms were barely heated, if at all. One of the most enjoyable outdoor jobs was grooming the horses. They enjoyed being brushed and fed, and I liked doing this when they were brought into the stable, which they preferred over the paddock, especially in winter. My love of horses began at Battle House. They were not ridden very often, but occasionally the Dunns hosted a foxhunt. On the scheduled day, the courtyard swarmed with horses, and dogs were underfoot everywhere. The dark-colored horses and white-spotted dogs made a lively collage. Soon they were off to hunt, but, the time that I was there, their intended prey "outfoxed" them all, and I liked that.

I celebrated my first Christmas in England at Battle House, where I shared a room with Pierre, the oldest of the Dunn children. Waking up on Christmas morning we found many presents at the foot of our beds. This was a cornucopia I didn't expect, so different from the stocking filled with coal, onions, and just a few small presents I was used to receiving at home on St. Nicholas Day, which we celebrated on December 6. The origin of giving gifts to children who were good, and coal to children who had been bad, goes back to the legend about St. Nicholas from the Orthodox Christian tradition. But in Czechoslovakia, as elsewhere in Eastern Europe, it was a national tradition that Jewish as well as Christian families participated in.

When spring arrived, tending the kitchen garden was added to my chores. I harvested the vegetables in season and brought them to the kitchen. The garden had every type of vegetable, including leeks, artichokes, turnips, and other growing things I had never seen or tasted. It always made me think of the Garden of Eden, and it inspired me to try my hand at "farming" on a smaller scale by planting my own vegetable and flower patch on another part of the property. I was proud of my efforts when I gathered a respectable harvest from my plot. Apples from the orchard were stored in an outside cold-storage shed, and for the first time I enjoyed eating good crisp apples all winter. I realized I was starting to like life on a farm.

Later in my stay I moved in with the older Austin boys, into a large bedroom in the old section of the house. The room had a low ceiling with exposed wood beams and a creaky sloping floor, an ideal setting for the ghost stories we heard and told. When I became ill the next year with appendicitis, I was moved into one of the two guest bedrooms at the front of the house. There in the bookcase I found Agatha Christie's *Murder in Mesopotamia* featuring Hercule Poirot—and so began my life-long interest in the adventures of the little Belgian.

As I became integrated into the routine of the Dunn household, the history of the place that was my temporary home interested me more. I appreciated the naming of Battle House when I learned the old part of the house dated from the sixteenth century; it was said that Oliver Cromwell, in the years he was fighting to overthrow the English monarchy, slept in the same timber-ceiling room that I occupied for a time. But in retrospect, Cromwell was probably reputed to have slept in as many different houses in England as George Washington in America! The spacious attic, a great place for us children to sneak away and hide, might once, I imagined, have stored mysterious treasures from past centuries, and if one didn't look down, a climb out on the parapet that encircled the outside of the house was a great thrill.

Mother tutored the three younger children in the nursery, and sometimes I participated, but more often than not I was helping Mr. Duck. As my scope of contacts widened, I became aware of the rivalry between Mrs. Dunn of Battle House and the vicar of the parish church who lived at the vicarage, the only other large house in the village. The vicarage, built of cold gray stone with an imposing front door, looked forbidding. I frequently banged the knocker on that door because it was there that I was sent to supplement my lessons in geography and other subjects.

The vicar was the Rev. Mr. Phillips, a well-educated, austere looking middle-aged man. He and Mrs. Dunn were either on good terms or at dagger points with each other, depending, perhaps, on the alignment of the stars or some other obscure reason. During one of the favorable periods in their relationship, someone suggested I be released temporarily from my chores at Battle House so Mr. Phillips could tutor me. Each week I took the fifteen-minute walk to the vicarage where Mrs. Phillips, who was much younger than her husband, greeted me and later breezed in with a plate of cookies. One day Mr. Phillips invited me to join the boys' choir since I had a good soprano voice and liked to sing. I proudly became the fourth choirboy in the Church of England services. When Mrs. Dunn saw me robed and proceeding down the church aisle, she exuded loudly, "Doesn't he look angelic!" Arriving at my seat in the choir, this "angel" was pleased to notice a perfect observation view of the girls' choir dressed in their Sunday best, unencumbered by the heavy robes of us boys. I passed the time looking at them during the long sermons that I did not understand.

American troops began to arrive in Britain in 1942 and some were stationed nearby. The village decided to invite these servicemen for tea and a social, but where should such a noteworthy event be held? Mr. Phillips thought the large grounds of the vicarage were the logical spot, but Mrs. Dunn wanted it at Battle House. Everyone at Battle House was excited when Mrs. Dunn prevailed, but the downside to her victory was that massive preparations had to be made in very short order. The large lawn was to be trimmed, manicured, and precisely cut with a hand-mower, now vintage of course. The flower beds had to be weeded, the bushes trimmed and shaped, and the driveway perfectly raked. For days before the appointed hour, Mr. Duck and I worked steadily and looked for ways to make sure everything was spiffy for the GI's. When the Americans came, they came in droves, a few hundred of them it seemed to me, and their lounging bodies covered the expansive lawns. I wondered if they were aware of our intense beautification efforts. This was my first exposure to people with dark skin since there were some among the soldiers, and I could not help staring at them, curious what made them so and wondering what they were like. They seemed the same as everyone else.

By the end of 1941, the Battle of Britain had been won and the nightly bombings of London had ended. My stay at Battle House lasted a little more than a year, and then I was sent to the boarding school for refugees organized by the Czech government in exile. For whatever reason, Mrs. Dunn decided to buy a house in London and move to town. The town house was a couple of blocks from Buckingham Palace and convenient to almost everything, so perhaps that was the reason. Mother moved with the family to London, and whenever I was on holiday from my boarding school I visited my parents in London and stayed at the Dunn's town house. The following year, Mother took a position as secretary with the Czechoslovak government in exile and served Czech leaders Hubert Ripka and Ivo Ducháček. When she moved out of the town house, my relationship was severed with the Dunn family and Battle House. I have often wondered what happened to all those Dunns because, unfortunately, we lost contact. I remember my days at Battle House fondly as some of the happiest ones of my stay in England.

Forty-five years later, in 1985, I returned to England with my wife to visit places I lived during the war. As we drove up the long driveway to Battle House, we saw row upon row of Quonset huts and greenhouses where lawns had once adorned the property. The paddock now had no horses, only the huts. The house seemed to me to have shrunk since 1942 when I was living there as a boy. I rang the doorbell at the familiar entrance and met the lady who answered and now owned the house with her husband. She invited us in and was joined later by her husband. To my great surprise, he was also a Czech. He settled in England after serving in the Royal Air Force and later married this English woman. Together they ran a horticultural business with the plants grown on the property. Much had changed there, and when the visit was over I decided that I prefer to remember the Battle House of my boyhood.

One evening when I was visiting my parents in London in 1942, we attended a gathering of fellow Czechs. A recording of Bedřich Smetana's *Vltava* (The Moldau), a reminder of Vltava River, which flows through

Prague, was played in complete silence, punctuated only by barely suppressed sobs as each person now in exile recalled happier days in our homeland. The deep emotion that permeated the room moved me and increased my own homesickness for my country. I was a boy who wondered what lay ahead for me, what was I alive for, and how the purpose of my life would evolve.

Chapter Five: From School to School to School, 1939–1944

———————◆———————

ATTENDING FIVE DIFFERENT schools in eighteen months because of my many moves that year is not the usual prescription for a good education, but that is how many I attended, and these schools provided me with my academic foundation for life.

When I arrived on the Kindertransport in London in May 1939, I was immediately enrolled at the local elementary school even though my knowledge of English was almost nonexistent. My fluency in the new language greatly improved during the summer when I played with other children at the seaside. Shortly after school resumed I was evacuated to Northampton, and there I attended the local school for only two months before I was reunited with my mother. Together we moved into the Dunn family residence. I was starting to be a little more confident speaking English; however, I did not attend any school right away, and I was delighted by another holiday so soon after the one in Ramsgate during the summer.

My distinctly accented English marked me as "foreign." In the past I had not considered nationality to be my primary identity, but now I was being called the "Czech Boy." I was proud of my country and knew that it had been victimized by Hitler, so I accepted the new designation, which neither offended nor thrilled me.

As I adapted more to English culture, I tended not to disclose my personal history even though my Czech heritage remained an integral part of me. How many times I contemplated the question, "Should I open up to new people I meet and tell my background, perhaps adding some information about my home country, or should I keep quiet and let them guess the origin of my accent?" I most often chose silence for fear of appearing to exploit my past, perhaps as a reaction against my occasional earlier exaggerations or maybe because that was the easier path for someone naturally shy.

For my mother, the school further away always seemed better than the one nearby: the educational grass was always greener on the other side of our fence. The first time I noted this quirk in her was in Bromham, Wiltshire, when I came to live at Battle House. My education was directed by Mother. The local school was a five-minute walk away, but I had to attend the school in the next village. Every morning that cold winter, I bundled up and set out walking across the fields, traversing one to another by climbing over wooden stiles sometimes covered with snow, then arriving exhausted and nearly frozen at the two-room schoolhouse. Usually the iron stove in each room was going full blast, so thankfully it was cozily warm inside. Once thawed out, I forgot the arduous trek to get there until it was time to go home.

Before walking back the same way, I often diverted to make a favorite stop. Opposite the school was a little shoe repair shop where sometimes I took shoes to be mended. I found the cobbler likeable and, seeking companionship, often stopped by even when I didn't bring him any business. My visits to the cobbler increased, and over time I stayed longer. As I looked around his tiny workshop, I was impressed with how neat everything was; he knew where each tool belonged, and they were always returned to their designated place. We talked more and more frequently as he continued to work. I was pleased that he was interested in my story, and I was glad when he encouraged me to develop it for him in detail. I described my happy times in Czechoslovakia and told him about my present life in the big manor house where Mother and I now lived. Even being shy, I felt no reluctance in conversing with the cobbler—conversation flowed easily between us. He told me about life in his village, how he became a cobbler, and described his military service in France during the previous Great War, vividly recalling several battles. The cobbler and I thought how ironic it was that we should now be in another world conflict with the same enemy he had fought not long ago! I felt the cobbler was my true friend, and much later I reflected on how, at this time of preadolescence insecurity, he had provided somewhat of a comforting substitute father figure for me.

The hardworking cobbler also encouraged me, especially when it came time to sit for the exam to be admitted to the academic high school, for which I felt unprepared. I failed the exam with a score of eighty-nine, needing one hundred to pass. I was tripped up on several questions because I did not know the difference between the time designations of a.m. and p.m. as this had not been taught in my classes. But I took comfort that the other three students taking the same exam had a *combined* score of eighty-one. Even though I had done considerably better than they had, I was disappointed in myself; and as a result of my score that autumn, I was forced to attend the trade school in Calne which required a half-hour ride by bus and ended the pleasant visits to my cobbler friend. But I continued to think fondly of him.

At the trade school I had my first brush with real danger. When the air raid siren sounded, we all scurried under our desks as we had been drilled to do. One time when we heard the planes approaching there followed a sharp rat-tat-tat and suddenly shattered glass clattered around us and fell all over the room, covering desktops and floor. We realized the Germans were machine-gunning the school. We were more terrified than we had ever been—luckily, though, no one was hurt. The next night a German plane dropped a bomb that landed in the field next to the meadow in our village and created a huge crater. Once our fear subsided, everyone was curious, so we all went cautiously to inspect it the following day.

Before the autumn of 1940 was over, I was preparing again to move to a new school—this time to attend the boarding school that the Czechoslovak government in exile in England was starting for the children of Czech refugees. Located near London, the building was well suited to be transformed into a school with dormitories, classrooms, and dining facilities in place. But this year was also the height of the blitz, and every night we heard the relentless droning of Nazi planes on their way to London with their deadly loads of explosives. That was very unsettling to me.

I developed one very positive lifelong habit at the Czech school: daily exercise. Each morning, no matter how cold and damp the weather, we students were herded out for calisthenics in the frigid air to do prescribed stretches, bends, and exercises. The set routine of physical exercise in the morning has stuck with me throughout my lifetime with only some adjustments for age—but in my bedroom or a gym setting, not outdoors!

The best news for students in that school year was the announcement in December that the British government had requisitioned our building and we would have no school to attend for a couple of months. Again I had free time to help the gardener at Battle House and continue to build a love for growing things. The interruption was necessary in order to create classrooms, dormitories, and bathrooms out of a large private residence called Hinton Hall by tearing down walls and constructing partitions. These changes transformed this country manor into our new school. Located in Whitchurch, Shropshire, Hinton Hall was a working farm run by a Mrs. Lewis and her two sons. Some of the older boys at our school were recruited to work toward getting the building ready and there was much dismay when one of them climbed out clandestinely onto a second floor stone balcony that gave way. He suffered a broken leg which reinforced for the rest of us the rule we often ignored—not to climb on places where we were not allowed to be.

I had many good times during the two years I lived at Hinton Hall. The train ride from Wiltshire to Whitchurch took all day and I usually rode alone, but the countryside was peaceful and there were no air raids. Hinton Hall was a three-story brownstone building with numerous nooks and crannies that were a delight for boys to explore. Many things there were makeshift to serve as a school. Although I don't remember much about specific classes, I do recall that my first year classroom had a working fireplace, unusual for a school. It added a homey feeling to the surroundings that I liked.

A few of us trapped rabbits on the grounds around Hinton Hall to supplement our diets, although we were never really hungry. Early in the morning we would charge out to see if we had caught anything, and if we had we would roast the meat on a spit over an open fire and enjoy the perception of ourselves as grown-up manly hunters.

A rabbi came to the school from London each week to provide us Jewish kids with religious instruction. I attended as a matter of course, but none of the teaching made much of an impression on me. I was at full attention, however, with some other events at the school held outside of regular classes. I recall great anticipation when Edvard Beneš, the Czechoslovak president in exile, honored us with a personal appearance, and, of course, there was endless preparation for this state visit. Beneš, a slight man, waved at us as he stepped out of his limousine and walked toward the stairs. We students were lined up on the grand stone staircase entrance, tense but ready to sing Czech folk songs for him, which we had rehearsed for weeks.

The Lewis family continued to live at Hinton Hall while we were there. The younger son, John, ran the farm, while his older brother, Bill, was in the British army. One of the persistent great mysteries at Hinton Hall was that small quantities of food were often disappearing. The kitchen was in the basement and food was transported to the dining room by means of a dumbwaiter. There was an intervening floor between the two and it was rumored that Mrs. Lewis would sometimes ease the chore of cooking dinner for her family by short stopping the loaded dumbwaiter and taking off already prepared morsels. Despite our detective work, we never found out if this was actually true.

Whitchurch was a small town about a forty-minute walk from Hinton Hall, and a group of us students would walk to town almost every Saturday. I loved to visit the bookstore, but since my financial resources were very limited, I was always tempted to help myself and several times actually walked away with some volume under my jacket.

Eventually I was caught and after a severe lecture by the school principal I vowed to him and myself that I was cured of stealing for good.

At this time I got to know my brother somewhat better. Frank, who by then was in the Czechoslovak army, was stationed in Whitchurch for a brief period while completing his gymnasium diploma. It was fun to suddenly have him close-by, and I got to meet several of his army buddies, which made me feel very grown up. I was quite proud of Frank, especially when I saw him in his dress uniform. One Saturday as I was walking into town, I saw Frank at the roundabout outside of town, hitchhiking. I ran up to him, "Where are you going?" I asked.

"To Manchester."

"Why?" I pressed.

A vague look came over Frank's face and he remained silent as if he had forgotten I was there. After a pause he looked at me and responded evasively, "I'll tell you when you're older." Naturally, my boy's imagination took off in high gear, but something told me to drop the subject and I just said, "Well, I'll see you."

Although I was happy at Hinton Hall and doing well in school, Mother decided that as long as we were in England I should get a "proper" English education. She secured a scholarship for me at Fulneck Boys' School located in Pudsey, Yorkshire, north of London between the cities of Leeds and Bradford. The school was operated by the Moravian Church, which is a small Protestant Christian denomination that pre-dates the Reformation. Founded in the aftermath of the burning at the stake in 1415 of Jan Hus, the Czech reformer, the Moravians grew substantially in number in Bohemia and Moravia, in the Czech Republic, until in 1620 the Catholic Counter-Reformation sent it underground. Its last bishop was John Amos Comenius, a celebrated educator known as the father of modern education. His book, *Didactica Magna*, advocated for universal education and introduced illustrated textbooks as well as logical thinking instead of rote memorization. For these concepts he was a candidate for the first presidency of Harvard College. The Moravian Church had a rebirth in the early eighteenth century in Saxony and its missionaries brought it to America.

In the fall of 1942, along with a boy who was already attending Fulneck, my mother saw me off on another train journey—this time a ride of five hours to Leeds. We transferred to a bus and were let off at the end of a long street that was the beginning of the Moravian settlement called Fulneck. The Moravians turned out to have a great influence on my inner struggles as a boy in England as well as on important later life decisions in America.

The Fulneck Moravian settlement was situated on a hill on one side of the main street opposite a row of little stone cottages. Further on three-story school buildings became visible. In the center of the complex was a structure with a small steeple, identifying it as the church—the focal point of the community. By descending a long, steep staircase, the girls' school appeared on the left and the boys' on the right. The only time we boys saw the girls was at special school performances held at the girls' school and when the girls marched into the church on Sunday mornings. The boys always arrived ahead of the girls—so we were afforded a better view of them as they filed in and sat down. Some older boys liked to tell of clandestine visits to see the girls, their stories most likely richly embellished with wishful thinking. But we younger boys always gave them our rapt attention, believing everything we heard.

The next two years at Fulneck were for me happy and fulfilling. Academically and socially I learned and grew. We slept in a large unheated dormitory with four rows of beds and windows open wide even in winter. If a boy was next to a window, as I was for a time, the snow would settle on the thick layer of blankets on the bed. If one did not get up immediately when called, the prefect (an older student appointed to maintain order) would take the blankets and rip them off the bed in one stroke. The prefect had to rise early each morning in order to perform his sadistic duties at the right time and thoroughly.

We had certain privileges. Every Saturday we boys lined up on the sidewalk, and when the master (the teacher in charge) gave the signal, we all ran at top speed to the neighborhood candy store, about a block away, to spend our weekly allowance. Once there, I faced impossible decisions of my pre-diabetic days—what to buy? Should I get my favorite, a Milky Way, or several pieces of penny candy that last longer? Or perhaps a chocolate bar? Or toffees? I loved them all and wanted them all, but like the others I had only sixpence to spend. It was agony to figure out how to get the most and use up all the money, and there was a press of the other boys—all of us facing similar dilemmas. In our impatience it seemed to take ages to get waited on, and if I, or another, was still undecided, the shopkeeper would turn away to wait on some-one who had made up his mind. She had to move fast with a mob in her store. Once finally outside with my loot, I would mentally taste the various flavors in my bag before choosing one and popping it into my mouth. The problem was always what to eat immediately and what to save for later. I reminded myself that my supply of delicacies had to last all week, until we reenacted the same ritual the following Saturday.

Students were allowed to walk into town, although there was little to do there. My special destination was the firehouse. I was working for a Boy Scouts merit badge in firefighting and part of the requirement was to become familiar with fire engines and firemen. The men treated me wonderfully and let me slide down the pole as they did when going to a fire. Although I could not accompany them on a real call, I loved to hang around the station and listen to the firemen's shouts and chatter.

Sports were a daily part of each school day at Fulneck. In the fall and winter we played field hockey and soccer outdoors in all kinds of weather. I hated field hockey but was passionate about football (soccer) and was proud to become a quite passable goalie. In the spring and sum-mer it was cricket and tennis. But since cricket was so strange to me, nobody wanted me on their team; I was relegated to scorekeeper, where I was at least able to learn the rules of the game well. Since my days as a younger boy hanging around the courts in Prague, tennis had been the sport that captured my interest and that I was best at. I was particularly proud when on one occasion the masters invited me to play with them as they needed a fourth for doubles.

The teachers at Fulneck were numerically small for the hundred or so boys enrolled—but all are unforgettable to me. Mr. Shaw, the science teacher, was lanky, stern, and unsmiling but became a hero in our eyes when we learned that he had saved a boy's life. The story circulated of how the boy unwittingly touched a downed power line and might have been electrocuted to death but for the quick thinking and instant action of Mr. Shaw who ran to him, took off the rubber boots he was wearing, and using them as gloves, with great difficulty extricated the frightened boy. The right teacher in the right place at the right time.

Then there was rotund Mr. Taylor, the headmaster, who seemed to us to be almost as wide as he was tall. Consistent with his round frame was a chubby face accentuated by puffy jowls and a ruddy complexion. We decided to christen him Tubby, an accurate moniker. But we were wary of Tubby as he often prowled the hallways and invariably discovered us if we were somewhere we were not supposed to be. I had respect for Tubby, though. I remember his broad smiling face when, at the end of the first school year, he handed me a book, *The Oxford Book of Light Verse*, the prize for "General Progress." I felt honored and pleased that Mr. Taylor appeared genuinely proud of me.

But the most unforgettable faculty member at Fulneck was Mr. LaTrobe, who taught geography and French and was called Toby by all of us when he was out of earshot. He appeared ancient—at least ninety-five years old, we thought. Probably his disheveled appearance aged him; he always looked as if he had just rolled out of bed. His fly was frequently unzipped, to the amusement of all of us, and his pants were so baggy that we made bets on when they would fall off in class. Toby was essentially bald but for a few gray wisps that protruded from the sides of his head and appeared to be an extension of his large ears. We marveled at how his polished pate shone and how it contrasted with the disorder of the rest of him. For me Toby comes to mind whenever I see a production of *Falstaff*. But for all his oddities he knew his stuff, and he kindled within me a lasting interest in geography.

I also still recall the athletic figure of Mr. Basil MacLeavy who taught Latin. A tall, well-built man, he exuded an air of confidence. He always stood erect, shoulders back, with a stern expression on his uncreased face as he paced in front of us listening to our declensions and halting translations. Mr. MacLeavy displayed a more human, less forbidding face when a fourth player was needed for tennis doubles and I was recruited. On the court I witnessed Mr. M. get very angry each time he netted the ball, and I suspected that a word unfit to be uttered by a master might have escaped his lips.

My second year at Fulneck began with exciting news that kept us all abuzz. Two new faculty members had been added, and, in a break from the traditional all-male teaching staff, they were women. Both were young, and one, Miss Vera Black, the English teacher, became my favorite. I was impressed with her curly jet black hair, which framed a plain but kindly round face. Her distinguishing feature to me was her broad, sincere smile. Some of the boys were almost as tall as she and her rather plump figure accentuated her short stature. But infatuation on my part completely overcame any physical imperfections she may have had, and I looked forward to sitting by her side in the library as she corrected my essays. The library was a small room lined with books completely covering the walls. It had that unique and pleasing smell of old seasoned volumes. I often sat at one of the tables next to Miss Black as she showed me how to improve my prose and taught me the meanings of English words unfamiliar to me and unrelated to my native language. I even recall learning from her the difference between 'reverberations' and 'repercussions.' Later I learned that Miss Black married our Latin teacher and became Mrs. Basil MacLeavy, and that the couple moved to Jamaica and taught school there.

Report cards at Fulneck always included comments by the masters. Once my report card had the comment "Ivan tends to be morose." I rushed to the dictionary to find the meaning of that word morose, as it was unknown to me. The definition was "gloomy or sullenly ill-humored." Was that *really* me? I was stunned—this was not how I would have described myself, but I started to wonder about others and if they might also wrongly consider me morose. I continued to dwell on the comment, becoming temporarily depressed by it and then angry at what I considered an unwarranted observation. Thinking about the meaning of morose filled me with self-doubt, and the comment still rankles me today, seventy-plus years later. Over the years I have occasionally composed a defense in my mind against the master who wrote "tends to be morose"—as if we were in a court of law. I would begin by saying, "Consider that in the year 1943 a war was raging. I was separated from my parents, and my brother was in the army fighting our enemy. Many of my relatives, including my grandparents, remained in danger in German-occupied Czechoslovakia, and I had been forced to flee my homeland." I would ask to be viewed as a boy with a lot on my mind. Was I ill-humored? I knew I was serious and I did feel somewhat out-of-place among all the English boys attending the school. I never minded being alone, though, and I was not a loner, having made several friends. I did my schoolwork conscientiously and I received the Book Prize for General Progress. Yes, I would admit to the Court, in those days I was dreadfully shy and thus often kept quiet because small talk, especially, was difficult. My present self would bring the Court up to date: "It took many years into adulthood to overcome shyness and gain self-confidence. Perhaps being an introvert made me appear to this teacher as moody. I would categorically reject the 'morose' label both then and now. I rest my case, your Honor."

Every day at Fulneck we had to attend morning and evening prayers as well as two church services on Sunday. It was a routine that became increasingly meaningful to me. Gradually I began to feel that a higher power was in control of the world and that everything was ultimately going to turn out well. I found the thought comforting. At Fulneck I also found a community that accepted me and expressed care and concern even though its strict behavioral discipline was not always appreciated. After a year of religious exposure I wanted to be a part of this community. I discussed my desire to become a Christian with my parents. Although Mother gave me tacit approval, I could tell Father was strongly opposed. At the time I did not consider what a blow my adolescent independence must have been to my father, although I don't recall that he openly conveyed his feelings to me. Perhaps he debated, even agonized, about whether to reproach me for what he was feeling, but he did not. I decided to go ahead anyway, received instruction, and was baptized on March 22, 1944. I distinctly did not consider this act a betrayal of my Jewish heritage. After all, I told myself, wasn't Jesus a Jew? Under religious and academic tutelage at the Fulneck School in those formative years, I started to define the purpose for my life that I had been seeking. This yet-to-be-defined goal had less to do with my own desires but was more directed toward a broader outlook for a life that would focus on benefiting others.

On weekends we could obtain permission to visit families overnight. One weekend I was invited to the home of a family in Leeds whose name was Bull. I found my way there by means of a bus and trolley through dingy streets to the unpretentious house of these working people. On the way I passed the burnt-out remains of Kirkstall Abbey and was fascinated by the image of monks living and working there many centuries ago. The abbey ruins stood as a grim reminder of Henry VIII's excesses, which we learned about in school. The Bull family had a boy my age, and we became good friends during my several visits. We played soccer with his pals and Whist (a card game) with the entire family participating in the evening. Without exception, members of the extended family were warm and friendly, and I realized how generous they were when Mrs. Bull passed me a plate with ten bacon strips and told me that was their weekly ration for the household. She clearly wanted me to feel like a member of her family.

Vacations posed a problem. What was a teenage boy to do on school vacations when there was no real home to return to? My parents were now living in London, in a rooming house during the war years, and I slept on a couch when I visited them. Even if that was an acceptable arrangement for a few days, what was I to do for two long summer months? Facing that situation I decided to pursue my interest in farming by volunteering to harvest crops in manpower-stressed England. I was only fourteen, but farms were short-handed and I hoped to be accepted as a farm worker.

Fortunately, my father knew someone at the Baťa Shoe Company, which had a factory and a farm in a rural part of the country. Baťa was a large shoe manufacturer that began in Zlín, in the Czech Republic and expanded to various parts of the world, including England and Canada.

I took a train to the farm work destination and walked to a dormitory where I was to stay with other workers from the Baťa enterprise. I was assigned a small room all to myself, ate in the cafeteria, and each morning walked to the farm, where I was given a variety of assignments. My favorite task was to feed the animals—chickens, pigs, and especially horses, which I had become fond of tending at Battle House. Before supper I returned to the dorm, ate, and then what? I had time on my hands and there was nothing to do—no radio, no television, nothing. I read sometimes, but I could not do that for hours every evening. I was bored. I went on walks but found I was very lonely. With no one my age to pal around with, I was glad when that summer passed and I could return to school, to friends, and to a less self-focused, more eventful life.

Looking forward to the next summer, I was determined to find a more satisfactory situation. I still wanted to work on a farm and there remained a great need for laborers, even teenage help. I joined a pacifist-leaning organization called The International Volunteers in the Service of Peace that had started before the war in Switzerland. Work camps were organized by IVSP for young people like myself, and I was eager to begin my first stint during Easter break near Sheffield digging ditches with two other boys. We lived together in one room for two weeks, became good friends, and worked hard during the day, but when the vacation was over we never saw each other again. Disappointed, I became aware of how transitory friendships could be and learned how much they seemed to depend upon physical proximity.

That summer I continued with IVSP at a camp in Lincolnshire where some thirty of us, boys and girls, worked on a large farm. The crop I remember harvesting most is potatoes. Long rows of them had to first be uncovered from the soil, then individual potatoes were searched for by hand and put into sacks. At the closing time of one work day, we were nearly finished with one field but still had a couple of rows to go. There were about ten of us on this work detail and most wanted to stop and start next day with the incomplete rows. But I spoke up, surprising myself as I was one of the youngest in the group. "We have to finish the field. That's what is expected of us," I said with passion that rested on feigned authority. There was grumbling and my fellow workers must have wondered who I thought I was to order them around. Nevertheless, they continued to work and we finished the field. Later I wondered if this showed budding leadership qualities, like a strong sense of responsibility, or if it was just blind bullheadedness with a lucky outcome this time. Even today, once a task is defined I find it difficult to stop until the work is completed, a trait those who know me recognize.

My most deeply etched memories of the summer IVSP camp were of the social life. England enjoyed extended daylight because the country was on double daylight savings time: it stayed light until about ten o'clock. In these evenings we played games, among them chess, checkers, and table tennis. But the game I learned that summer that appealed to me most was spin the bottle. I had never kissed a girl on the lips before and found it especially pleasurable to be a winner at this particular game. After a while I found the courage to ask one of the prettiest girls to go for a walk. I thought we had become special friends, but I lost her a week later to an older, more confident, and socially adept boy. Romance, I learned, involved many challenges.

Then there was my laundry. The camp had no facilities for washing clothes so I made an arrangement to send my soiled clothes to the Bull family in Leeds who had befriended me earlier and whom I occasionally visited. Wrapping paper was at a premium during the war, so I always hoarded the best paper from packages I received and put it away for some special use at a later date. I wrapped my dirty laundry to send to Leeds in small, less desirable pieces of paper and held the packages together with string. Mrs. Bull finally wrote to inform me that my packages were arriving with the clothing sticking out of the parcels which came through with almost no paper covering. Humiliated, from then on I used my best wrapping paper for laundry packages. The lesson I learned was not to store away all the best things with the intention of saving them for some undefined future contingency.

I will never forget visiting Lincoln Cathedral on one of our days off from the camp. The bus ride was long but worth it. The cathedral is perched magnificently on the crest of a hill and dominates the town. As

I approached, it came into sharper focus, and I was overwhelmed by the stonework on one of the largest structures I had ever seen. I spent a great deal of time making a study of the intricate carvings that so impressed me all across the wide west wall below the two towers. This was such an unforgettable memory to me that I had to put the cathedral at Lincoln at the top of my itinerary when I visited the UK again years later.

When I was preparing to leave Fulneck, I visited the Bulls to say my good-byes and promised to write, but I never did. I don't know why I cut off this contact, but I regret now that I did and feel guilty. Experiences at the Moravian school meant so much to me that before I left I decided I needed a permanent memento to take with me. I noticed an impressive aerial photograph on a wall that showed the whole community and I coveted it. My earlier promise to the school principal in the bookstore incident and my personal vow at that time to never steal again were shelved for the time being. I stuck the framed photograph in my suitcase and lovingly hung it in all future rooms I lived in. But, eventually, I developed severe pangs of guilt about taking the picture, so when I visited England in 1985 and planned to visit Fulneck, I packed it again, to go back. Later I handed it over to the current headmaster who was very glad to receive it. I also gave him a sizable check which served as penance.

By the summer of 1944, it was clear to my parents that the Allies would defeat Germany and equally obvious to them that life in post-war Czechoslovakia would be very difficult. They decided to immigrate to the United States, where we already had family, and applied for our visas. Anticipating with growing excitement a new adventure ahead, I accompanied my parents to the US embassy in London and was being interviewed when a loud siren warned that a V-2 rocket was on its way. I followed the interviewer and we both ducked under a desk. We were obviously relieved when the "all clear" sounded, and after a couple of minutes the interview continued. As soon as our visas were received, we booked passage for the voyage we hoped would deliver us safely to America. In October 1944, my Fulneck headmaster accompanied me to Leeds and put me on the train for Liverpool, where I was to meet my parents to board the ship.

Chapter Six: Perilous Voyage to America, 1944

———————◆———————

W E WERE ON the move again, like prey seeking a safe haven. In the gathering dusk the silhouette of our ship was barely visible. I was a boy of fifteen who had never been on a large boat except for the ferry that transported me across the English Channel. I looked forward to being on this vessel, which was to carry the three of us from England to America and a new life. Frank, my brother, had volunteered for the Czechoslovak army in England when war broke out and was by this time at the front in France.

As my parents and I walked slowly up the gangplank, I saw a friendly face above, smiling and wearing a crisp white uniform. Looking at the passenger list on his clipboard, he gave us a hearty, "Welcome aboard, mates." He was short, balding, a little on the pudgy side, and introduced himself as Bill. I liked him at once. He told us he was the medical orderly on our ship, the S.S. Beaverhill. We told him our names, and I quietly volunteered, "We came from Czechoslovakia in 1939."

"Let me show you to your cabin," Bill offered. The cabin proved to be the size of a large bathroom with just enough room for two upper and lower bunks, a washbasin, and a small closet. On one of the lower bunks sat Mrs. Bassová, a compatriot and an acquaintance of my parents. She was their age, on the plump side with reddish hair, decidedly plain, and obviously disgruntled.

"How can four of us live in here for two weeks?" she complained immediately. Glaring at me she added, "There isn't enough room to even turn around and I won't have any privacy at all!"

Bill tried to cut through the tension by explaining, "Unfortunately, this is a cargo ship and there are only twelve passengers on board, and if it were not for the war there wouldn't be any of you here." Mrs. Bassová ignored him.

That night, as we prepared for bed, I began to understand what close quarters were going to mean. Mrs. Bassová barked out an order to me— "Turn your head and close your eyes so I can get in my nightgown and wash up." I shut my eyes as tightly as possible, thinking, "Who wants to look at *her* anyway?

The next morning I was up early and walked around on the deck stopping frequently to watch our ship cut effortlessly through the waves. During the night, a convoy had formed and there were ships about a quarter mile to port, to starboard, as well as fore and aft, and beyond them more ships all in neat rows. I was curious to know how many there were and went looking for Bill. "There are about seventy, including destroyers and cruisers that will protect us from U-boats," he told me. That was very reassuring.

"You want to see the rest of the ship? I'll show you around when I get some free time," Bill offered. I jumped at the chance, and at eleven o'clock I was ready and waiting at his door. He came out to announce there were only two patients that morning and they were both feeling bilious. I had never heard the word.

"What does bilious mean?" I asked.

"It's usually an upset stomach from being at sea," he replied, "but it covers everything imaginable when one is out of sorts—and that happens often to people not used to the motion."

We started our tour at the back of the ship, where I saw the cargo area first. The hold was full of large containers, but since everything was crated I couldn't see what cargo the ship was carrying. "The engine room may be more interesting to you," Bill continued, so we walked to the entrance of the hottest, noisiest, and most unpleasant part of the ship. Conversation in there was impossible.

I observed the convoy and asked, "How can you tell we are even moving since all the ships are always in the same position?"

"You'll know by tomorrow," he nodded with assurance. "Expect it to be much warmer because we're sailing southwest right into the Gulf Stream. We're going to zigzag across the Atlantic so that German U-boats don't detect us ... hopefully." It was his "hopefully" that made me uneasy. In the closing days of the trip we did hear depth charges exploding around us as our escort vessels warded off the dreaded submarines.

I felt I knew Bill pretty well by this time so I asked him directly, "Are you ever afraid being at sea all the time during the war?"

"Not very," he replied. "You get used to it and don't think about it too much." I could tell he didn't want to expand upon the topic I had raised when he abruptly transitioned into, "It's almost lunch time and I'm busy this afternoon, but after supper I'll show you some night sights. Meet me on deck about eight o'clock."

Later, as I looked around me, it was totally dark and I couldn't see the other ships. But I saw millions of white dots all around us—constellations, stars, planets. How thrilling for a budding astronomer like me! I couldn't make out where the sky ended and the sea began as everything blended into blackness, but the convoy plowed on. We were at the railing when Bill asked me, "Have you looked down?"

I did, immediately, and I answered with, "Look at that! All those little things that are lit up are bumping against the side of the ship—what are they?" Amused, Bill explained that they were phosphorescent particles found in the sea and at night they shone in this way.

"Then it's like the reflection of the stars in the water," I said with great excitement as if I alone had just discovered an eternal truth.

The next day I lingered on deck watching the ships when out of the corner of my eye I caught a glimpse of my cabinmate nemesis approaching. I scooted into a doorway in order to avoid Mrs. Bassová but was too late. "Ivan, come here," she bellowed, and like a shamed puppy I obeyed. "*Mě je* špatně," she spat out, meaning I am not well. "I need your friend the orderly," she continued. I saw my chance to escape and immediately set out to find Bill.

"What's the matter with her?" he asked.

"She's feeling bilious in a big way," I told him, proud of my seafaring vocabulary.

"Tell her to meet me in the dispensary right away," Bill directed.

I was relieved to be temporarily free of her; but, unfortunately, I was in our cabin alone when Mrs. Bassová returned. "Your friend was so nice to me," she cooed. "He gave me some pills and told me to stay in bed for a day. "But," she frowned, "how can I rest with all of you coming and going in here?" Hiding my delight at getting to leave, I told her I would gladly vacate so she could lie down.

And so the journey continued day by day. After a few days of balmy weather, it turned colder, and I knew we were heading north. Sometimes when he wasn't busy with health duties, Bill and I would talk about his experiences on various ships, and I described to him the boarding school I had just left. I learned about the seafaring life and was able to get away from the unpleasant Mrs. Bassová.

Conversations at meals were desultory, with only twelve passengers seated at two tables. But I remember one conversation well. It was a couple of days before the first Tuesday in November 1944, when Americans would choose between President Franklin D. Roosevelt and Thomas Dewey to be president of the United States for the next four years. "Roosevelt is our savior," my father declared more than once, "and without him America would not be in the war, and without America the allies would be finished." Another chimed in to agree. "How can you trust Dewey? He has no foreign policy experience." Election results came in slowly as we huddled around the radio. When it became clear that FDR had won a fourth term there was a loud "hooray" from both passengers and officers.

As we neared the end of the voyage I noted that my parents grew more pensive. I tried to read their thoughts beyond what they shared with me. Father was preoccupied with his ailing heart, wondering how he would support us. Mother was eager for our new country with its promise of opportunity, but she, too, had worries. How dominant would Father's older brother, Paul, be? He was sponsoring us in America, but would he try to interfere in our lives as well? I was mostly looking forward to being in America, my new country.

When we reached Saint John in New Brunswick, Canada, we said our good-byes. Bill had become my guide and a friend and contributed to making the trip memorable for me. "Good luck, mate," he waved as we disembarked. "Same to you, Bill," I shouted back.

A few weeks later in New York City we read that our ship went aground in the Saint John Harbour. The S.S. Beaverhill had an interesting history and a tragic end. It was one of five ships known as the "Beaver Class." These were general purpose vessels built in Scotland and registered in the Port of London. They were used for fast freight runs between Canada and the UK.

The SS Beaverhill was the last of this class of ships, the rest had been destroyed earlier by U-Boats and Luftwaffe bombers. It seemed to have had a charmed life, ferrying thousands of air force trainees across the Atlantic. In November of 1944 she steamed into Saint John, and its crew was given shore leave while longshoremen unloaded the ship. The ship was no stranger to Saint John, and her crew was familiar with winter sailing conditions in the Bay of Fundy as well as the mingling of Saint John River outflow and salt water tides.

The ship prepared for departure with a heavy cargo load in the early hours of November 24, 1944 as she had done many times before. She was being guided by a tug when suddenly the towing rope snapped and the loose end began to wrap itself around the propeller. The wind then pushed the ship onto Hilyard's Reef. When the tide receded, the damage that the S.S. Beaverhill had sustained opened wider and the ship cracked apart.

Chapter Seven: New York, 1944–1946

◆

ARRIVING IN New York City by train through the tunnel to Grand Central Station is the least picturesque way to enter this great metropolis; yet on a cloudy, chilly November day, that was how my parents and I first viewed the area about which I had heard so much and dreamed of experiencing. But the warmth of our human reception more than compensated for the inauspicious weather conditions when we arrived. Waiting on the platform were my Uncle Paul, Aunt Julia, and their daughter, my cousin Anna. I had not seen them for five long years, since they had left Prague already in March 1939, immediately after the Nazis occupied our country and two months before I boarded the Kindertransport train. We celebrated being together with a sumptuous supper at their apartment on 72nd street. The home-cooked meal was a special treat for me after eating only institutional food for the past few months at camp, at boarding school, and most recently on the ship.

My father, a diabetic, had not been well for some time, suffering from a heart ailment. Uncle Paul took charge of Father's health regimen by taking him to several doctors Paul selected and finally deciding Father should live, at least for the time being, with him and his family on 72nd Street. Mother and I were to live nearby. Mother agreed to conform to this plan and found a furnished room on 71st Street for the two of us. From 71st Street there was a convenient entrance to the 72nd Street apartment building, and we used it to visit Father every day and ate our evening meal there.

Living with my mother and my father, uncle, aunt, and cousin next door was altogether different from being in boarding school. I found Aunt Julia to be an overflowing fountain of love. Her enthusiasm and warmth was infectious and her concern for Father was touching. I liked that she could laugh at herself, especially when telling us her adventures of being constantly lost on the subway, and I found myself opening up to her. When Julia was a renowned singer in Europe in the 1920s and 1930s, she was performing in Prague as Cherubino in Mozart's *The Marriage of Figaro*. There is a scene in which Cherubino (the role is sung by a woman) is having "his" ears boxed. All of a sudden Paul, Julia's young son sitting in the audience, cried out, "Mother, DON'T LET HIM DO THAT TO YOU!" The audience broke into laughter.

I watched my Uncle Paul come home from the office every day, and promptly sit down with paper and pen to compose a letter to each of his sons who were in the army—Charlie in the Pacific and Paul in Italy. I was impressed with his commitment and consistency in writing to his sons. When Uncle Paul had to move his writing paraphernalia from one room to another, he would place the letters carefully on top of several folded newspapers to smooth out the paper. Observing this operation, it occurred to me that a big firm blotter pad would be an easier way for him to transport his letters, so I bought him one that first Christmas in America. I was overwhelmed by my uncle's response to my gift: he was very appreciative, thanking me more than once. One would have thought I had given him a brand new Cadillac.

I also responded with delight to again being in the company of my only girl cousin, Anna. She was a year older than I, studied at a private school, and had accumulated a wide network of girlfriends. Although Anna and I did not spend much time together then, I liked and admired her immensely, for her good looks and keen intellect as well as her friendly nature. She inherited her mother's generous disposition, showing love and acceptance to others and especially to her family. That trait continues to this day. Now, Anna and I see more of each other and enjoy a close relationship.

Modifications to my former life came almost daily. Uncle Paul suggested that we change our surnames, as his family had done, from Bächer with the umlaut over the "a," to just Backer. That sounded more American, he said. Naturally, we followed his counsel and became, as we are now, the Backers. I was happy not to have to explain umlauts and the correct spelling of my name.

The blending in this way of the two branches of our family was not without tension. My mother had worked earlier in London for the Czechoslovak government in exile. She intended to continue to work in America and had obtained a recommendation for a position at the Czechoslovak consulate in New York. She saw working at the consulate as a positive development since she liked financial independence and enjoyed interaction with others at a job. This precipitated the first family disagreement that I can recall. Uncle Paul was strongly opposed to her working, stating that her place was at home caring for the health needs of her husband. Nevertheless, Mother persisted and joined the staff at the consulate.

Uncle Paul took the responsibility of enrolling me in school. On the first Monday after our arrival he accompanied me to George Washington High School in Washington Heights. This was the school from which my cousins Charlie and Paul graduated, and he declared it was "the best." Once again I was to attend a school that was not close to where I lived—it required a forty-minute subway ride each way. When we arrived at the school and the principal reviewed my transcript from Fulneck Boys' School, he gave me an amazed and puzzled look, then declared, "You have enough subjects to be finished with high school right now, but you are not sixteen years old yet, so there is no way we can we let you graduate." This situation arose because in England I took nine subjects simultaneously, and in the US only five are taken at one time in high schools. No wonder I had completed all the requirements! I vividly remembered Mother emphasizing the value of a "proper"

English education and I understand now what motivated her to send me to Fulneck. Compromise needed to be reached with the principal, so it was decided I would attend high school there for a year plus a month and then be graduated. However, by the time the mid-year high school graduation exercises took place in January 1946, I was already in college, but apparently the principal didn't know this when he called out at graduating exercises, "Backer, Backer—*where is he?*" I never did receive my high school diploma to document that I graduated, but it didn't seem to matter.

George Washington High School was huge. My first day there was completely bewildering, especially since I was used to a school of about a hundred pupils and George Washington High had a staggering five thousand! Not only was the size of the school dramatically different, but there were girls there too, mixed into the student population with boys, and very different shades of brown skin were represented. I had seen a few black people as part of the American troops on the lawn at Battle House, and one in London's Regent's Park, and that was it. Now I was in class with many of them. Between courses I found the hallways to be a streaming mass of bustling bodies chattering noisily, and as I stood there confused, not knowing where to go next, a big African American boy put his arm on my shoulder and asked me, "Are you lost? Where do you want to go?" He showed me the way to my next class, and although I never recall seeing him again, from that moment on I lost any fear I may have had of black people. He never realized what a favor he had done me.

Once I went to Harlem. The 72nd Street Backers had occasional household help in the person of Evelyn, who cleaned and did some cooking. One time Evelyn was needed to carry something heavy home and I either volunteered or was volunteered to carry it for her. When we got off the subway at Lenox Avenue and 145th Street, I saw only black faces. I was fascinated with the naturalness of everyone going about his and her business. I was aware through discussions in England of the unjust and uneven treatment of black people in America, so the normalcy I saw surprised me. What struck me as odd was that when we arrived at the door of Evelyn's apartment, she had to unlock four locks to enter her small spotless home.

I began working Saturdays even before my sixteenth birthday, and my first employment was at an A.S. Beck shoe store on Delancey Street as a stock boy. I was fascinated with the street scene I sometimes saw outside the store. The unusual way Orthodox Jews dressed was novel to me, as was the price haggling prevalent among customers and peddlers behind their open stalls. Seeing the pushcarts and hearing the hawkers and chatter made me imagine I had landed on another planet. After I had been working at the shoe store for several weeks, I came to work one day as usual only to be told that I was no longer needed. I was surprised and then furious when I recalled it cost me a nickel on the subway to get there and I would need to spend another nickel to get back home yet the manager made no mention of this when he dismissed me. He also didn't say he was sorry or give me any encouragement whatsoever despite my hard work and perfect attendance. I calculated that a nickel was 10 percent of my hourly fifty-cent wage! Well, that was capitalism I growled to myself, and I definitely did not like being cast as the exploited worker.

But my next job I loved. Chain stores had a lock on their doors that recorded what time each day the manager opened and closed the shop. Once a week the paper that recorded the information, which was wound around a cylinder, had to be changed and a new paper put in its place. I had an established route of places to go where I had to change these recording strips. My route began at Rockefeller Center and wound through midtown, finishing on Tenth Avenue at the company office, where I turned in the paper strips I had removed earlier. One of my stops to which I looked forward eagerly was a candy factory where the receptionist supplied me with enough free candy to last all week.

One of my cherished dreams as a teenager was to be a farmer, the bug having bit me especially hard back in England during the two consecutive summers I worked on farms. Having specific responsibilities there made me feel grown up, and I especially enjoyed those work camps in England. When I came to America I continued my interest in farming. During the summers of 1945 and 1946 I worked near Hamilton, Ontario, in Canada on a farm operated by the Běhals, Czech refugees, who also employed three Czech hired hands. The Běhals were friends of my parents and, like me, escaped in 1939. To get to the farm job, I hitchhiked my way to Canada via Albany and Buffalo before the New York State Thruway was built and crossed on foot at Niagara Falls. One year I caught a ride all the way from Albany to Buffalo with a man in an old car who drove to the top of each hill on Route 20 and then cut off the motor and coasted down. I asked him why he did this and he said in order to save gas.

I had a great experience on the Běhals' farm. When I arrived in mid-June it was haying season. I liked riding on a big load of hay drawn by a pair of horses. On the way back from the barn to the field with an empty wagon, I found the horses were frequently frisky, and the challenge was to control them lest they run off with me. After the hay was in the barn, the wheat harvest came in August. Since all the farms were relatively small, 200 to 300 acres, no farmer owned his own threshing machine. When a rented thresher came to a particular farm, all the men from the neighboring farms would arrive to help so that all the grain grown on that farm would be threshed in one day. Everyone looked forward to the noon break because lunchtime was a veritable feast where each farmer's wife would try to set out a spread that outshone the previous wives' prepared lunches. These contests gave us something to talk about while working.

During the school year I continued farming in the New York borough of Queens where Queens College had an agricultural program. A couple of times a week I rode the subway from high school in Washington Heights in Manhattan to the end of the line in Flushing, about an hour's ride, and then walked to the farm. Although the ride was long, it gave me time to dream about the farm I planned to own one day and contemplate how I would run it. The Queens' farm included a variety of animals, so I picked up information on animal husbandry and also received instruction on pruning fruit trees. I felt I was storing away valuable information for my future. Eventually, however, my dream of farm ownership receded, but I have sometimes thought about what kind of farmer I would have been.

After the war, my cousins Charlie and Paul were discharged from military service. One cold day in December 1945, I was riding the 79th Street cross-town bus through Central Park. Paul had just come home, but I wasn't in contact with him yet; I thought how it had been six years since I last saw him. People were bundled in overcoats, hats, and scarves when a young man sat down next to me, leaning sideways toward a standing friend who was conversing with him. I stared—was this my cousin Paul sitting next to me? I wasn't sure and I thought it too bold to address him directly. I would be embarrassed if I spoke out and it wasn't Paul. So, instead, I took out a piece of paper and wrote in Czech, "Are you Paul? I am Ivan." I practically shoved it under his face then turned to look out the window. He finally read it and turned to me with great surprise and delight, "*You* are Ivan?" I turned red and acknowledged my identity. We were very glad to see each other again.

My love for New York City blossomed during that first year I lived there. I liked the independence it offered me, losing myself within its vastness, its tall buildings that towered overhead and the palpable, pulsating energy of the crowds. Anonymity in the city appealed to me, and I enjoyed the fact that no one knew me as I scurried here and there. I have never lost that sense of exhilaration, and it reawakens whenever I visit. The city continued to be my home for the next eight years. When my father's health improved, my parents and I moved into a two-bedroom furnished apartment on 69th Street (before Lincoln Center was built) and stayed there until 1947, when we moved to Washington Heights and lived at 105 Pinehurst Avenue. On vacations from college that remained my home base. The spacious five-room apartment was my mother's home until she died in 1984. In the meantime, Frank returned from Europe, where he had been escorting convoys bringing relief supplies to Czechoslovakia. Finally, all four members of our immediate family were together again.

Chapter Eight: Why Was I Spared? 1946–1952

———————————◆———————————

O N A COLD January day I carried my two well-worn suitcases to New York's Pennsylvania Station to catch a Lehigh Valley train to Bethlehem, Pennsylvania. I was off to Moravian College, the next rung on my educational ladder. Choosing Moravian came naturally, almost automatically, because of my positive experiences at the Moravian school at Fulneck, England. A generous scholarship from the college was further incentive to seal the deal.

I looked down at the half frozen brook meandering alongside the train tracks and thought about what lay ahead. Of course, it was not the first time in my young life I had traveled a train alone to an unknown destination, but in the earlier journeys arrangements were made for me and always included a person who would meet me at the end of the trip. Now I optimistically, but unrealistically, hoped someone would be sent by the college to direct me to my new place of residence. However, when the train pulled in and we disembarked, I stood on the platform and watched the other passengers walk away and disappear. Glancing around I quickly became aware there was no one to welcome me.

"How do I get to Moravian College?" I finally asked the clerk at the ticket office.

"Go up the stairs by the bridge, stay on this side of it, and take the bus up North Main Street." Sensing my confusion, he added, "Ask the driver to call out your stop." The voice wasn't particularly friendly.

I followed instructions, lugging my bags up many stairs to the bus stop. Stepping off the bus I found myself in front of a large gray stone building with two smaller colonial style structures across the street nearby. I wondered which was the right building then decided to walk the long path to the larger structure, which proved to be the right choice. Inside I was given information that my room was on the third floor and I would register for classes down on the first. I was proud to have dealt with transportation issues and orientation to a new, completely unfamiliar place entirely on my own for the first time.

The incoming class at Moravian College that year included 130 G.I. soldiers plus three of us who were newly minted high school graduates. I was sixteen and a half years old and had to face the challenge of conquering my fears and adapting to this unfamiliar environment. This new world I had entered seemed complex and confusing; I felt a total stranger in it. But I quit thinking so much about myself after I met my first roommate, and he told me about his army service in Europe. I listened to him and others who had been overseas relate stories about military life and give details of their exploits, especially sexual ones. I was jealous of their worldliness and well aware that I was being viewed for what I was—a schoolboy and a novice in matters concerning the opposite sex.

I attended the summer school session as did almost everyone else that first summer, and at age seventeen I became a sophomore. In my first semester at college I received what I considered one bad grade—a C in a compulsory gym class. The problem was with basketball, a game I had barely heard of and never played. I simply could not hit the basket! Nevertheless, most semesters I made the dean's list. Years later, at a college reunion, I was surprised that my classmates had labeled me "smart" although I hadn't thought of myself to be in any way exceptional.

I needed to supplement my college scholarship with jobs. My first work experience was sweeping dusty floors in the science building where renovations were underway. Later I worked in the dining room washing dishes and at the same time was employed as a soda jerk at the local luncheonette where I claimed banana splits as my specialty. Assisting Dr. Raymond Haupert, Moravian's president, in his garden was another occasional job, and, as in my earlier horticulture days, I liked working in the soil. In all these earning opportunities I made 50 cents per hour, and this money was my only source of funds.

Picking a major was no problem for me. I chose pre-med driven by my desire to be a medical missionary in Africa. That resolve had been nurtured by reading about Dr. Albert Schweitzer's life and investigating many of his writings. I determined in those early days at Moravian College that my life path was set, driven by my increasing and deepening desire to do something useful and serve others. I asked myself, isn't that what I was saved from the Holocaust for? I thought nothing was more worthwhile than to heal people in parts of the world where there were few doctors. During my first two years in college I took the requisite science courses and did well, although I was more drawn to the humanities, especially history.

At the same time I became friends with several students who were preparing for the Moravian Church ministry. The Moravian Theological Seminary shared the campus with Moravian College, and in my junior year it appointed a new dean. Soon after his arrival he called me into his office to ask me how I expected to be a medical missionary without any theological training. I told him my plan was to practice medicine first. I see now how the outcome of that meeting with the dean reflected my youthful age, natural shyness, and inexperience in defending myself. I was too immature to recognize and understand his bias when he launched into an argument with adult confidence to influence decisions about my future.

"You must first get a theological grounding! You can't be a missionary without being ordained and you can't be ordained without going to seminary," he insisted as a counter to my plan for starting with medical school. "After all," he continued, "you will only be twenty years old when you finish college and seminary takes just three years, so you will still be very young when you begin medical school."

I was facing a crossroad. At eighteen I found it difficult to argue with this man of authority who was such a smooth talker and compelling spokesman for the church. It is true, I thought, that three years is not that long. I never considered, nor did the dean, intervening events that might well arise over time in this broad outline of a young man's life and would derail the most distant part of the plan—medical school. I had feelings of doubt about what was being said to me, but reluctantly acquiesced and enrolled as a pre-theological student, but I still completed all my pre-med requirements. That trait from boyhood—to always finish what I start—was still with me!

I sought to attend a Moravian Church just as I had in England. There were five churches in the city of Bethlehem to choose from. Someone said that the best young people's group with the most girls was located at West Side Moravian Church. I wasted no time investigating this bit of news and in short order became a member of the group and sang in the church choir as well. The young people's group met every Sunday evening, and I found them extremely friendly and accepting of new members. Group discussions were intellectually stimulating to me, and often after the meetings all of us visited someone's house to enjoy refreshments. Gradually I felt at home here and became more confident socializing with girls.

That fall a new girl came to the young people's group. The first thing I noticed were her shapely legs, and as my eyes took in the rest of her I liked what I saw. Her name was Carolyn Bartholomew, but I was told to stay away from her because her fiancé died recently and that would mean she was in a fragile state. My heart sank but not for long as her grief lifted and we started dating a short time later. We shared a love of music—one of our favorite activities was attending the Community Concerts at Liberty High School, from which she had graduated. There we heard a very young Leonard Bernstein play and conduct one of Beethoven's piano concertos. Still bashful it took me ages to hold her hand and eventually to kiss her. I shouldn't have waited so long!

After I graduated from Moravian College in 1949 with a B.A. in History, I attended Moravian Theological Seminary for one year, concentrating on mastering Greek and Hebrew. I was on automatic learning pilot, going through the motions of learning but not enjoying it very much. A side issue that added to my discontent was being assigned a first attempt at teaching. With no prior preparation or warning, a fellow seminarian and I were told we would teach a bible class to fifty junior high students in after-school sessions at a church across town. The expected arrival of our students came to fill me with dread as I anticipated what would happen after they pushed and shoved their way through the narrow door into the room shouting and doing their best to show us they were uncontrollable mischief makers who were tired of teachers talking at them all day. We divided the unruly youthful mob into two groups and spent the next hour attempting to teach our half anything at all. I left each class feeling frustrated and deflated—not recognizing that in this situation we were set up for failure. We continued the charade for a year, and the situation never improved. If that was teaching, I knew it was not my calling. I decided that I needed more intellectual content, so I transferred to Union Theological Seminary in New York City. An incentive for moving to Union was Carolyn's presence there as she was studying for her master's degree in Sacred Music at Union's music school.

I thrived at Union and was especially stimulated by the lectures of Reinhold Niebuhr, Paul Tillich, James Muilenburg, and other leading thinkers. My understanding of the social dimensions of individual actions came into focus as well as the necessity for political and social action to effect meaningful change. Studying issues of social change and having an opportunity to share views with other students was what I needed and relished. My developing outlook played against my background of escaping the horrors of Nazi hatreds as well as reading recent revelations about the inaction of many civilians and religious leaders in the world, including in America, in taking a firm stand and act against the immense injustices of the time. I decided not to return to Moravian College and finished my Bachelor of Divinity degree at Union.

Between my second and final year at Union, Carolyn and I were married and we moved into the married students' dormitory at the seminary to begin our life together. My new bride and I lived in a small room where we slept on a hide-a-bed, cooked on a two-burner hotplate, and stored our perishables in a small ice chest. This was a new and exciting experience in basic living for both of us and we felt very independent. Every morning I crossed Claremont Avenue to the Seminary refectory to lug a large chunk of ice back for our ice chest. Since I had to carry it on my shoulder, I shivered all through breakfast.

Carolyn had earned a Masters of Sacred Music degree that year and began her career as a church musician at a Presbyterian church in Ridgewood, New Jersey. Her musical talent included a beautiful coloratura voice, and growing up she sang solos in churches. The last of her several voice teachers was my Aunt Julia, an opera star in Prague. When we moved to Yonkers, New York, in 1952, Carolyn and I both joined the Westchester Light Opera Company, an amateur group with high performance standards. I sang in the chorus, and when Mozart's *Magic Flute* was proposed, Carolyn, having a trained voice, was chosen to sing the difficult role of Queen of the Night. As it happened, she was nine months pregnant with our son on opening night. Baby Tim remained reluctant to face the world as Carolyn, very much past due at show time, donned her costume and prepared her voice. As I paced, the cast joked that an ambulance should be on call while she sang, but she performed her arias perfectly in a long, very full and flowing blue gown, which hid her quite large figure.

During my senior year at Union I did a great deal of soul searching. I struggled to recognize the life I was rescued for and agonized over defining my choices. I knew the upcoming decisions would guide the rest of my life and probably that of my family. In this period of ongoing confusion and inner turmoil, Union Seminary suggested a psychiatrist who became my counselor, supporter, and eventually friend. I was startled one day when I walked into Dr. Taylor's office and he told me he had been visited by Mother, but discretion prevented him from going into specific details. I was, of course, quite startled and immediately imagined the confrontation. I saw her starting with something like, "What are you doing with my son? You're taking him away from me!" I had no direct knowledge of what actually took place in the office, but I knew intuitively, supported by what Dr. Taylor felt he could disclose, that it was not a friendly meeting. I felt Mother was viewing me as the same vulnerable ten-year-old she put on the Kindertransport train to save my life years earlier. She sought to continue a motherly control into my adult life, which, in her view, remained her responsibility. I began to understand that this was a fight for my independence and future well-being, and I needed assistance to win the struggle. When Dr. Taylor and I no longer met for sessions, we corresponded with some regularity, tapering off to briefer holiday greetings once a year that were, nevertheless, meaningful to me and I believe to him. I mourned his passing in 2013 at age ninety-one.

In therapy I struggled to make some decisions. I concluded that in order to serve others I did not necessarily have to become a medical missionary in Africa. I understood that I had been driven earlier by mixed motives, and I gave up my intention to become a doctor even though I had been accepted at Temple University Medical School. I was still confused and floundering as graduation approached without my having any distinct plan for the future. However, I had decided not to enter the Moravian ministry and be responsible for a church as the Moravian Church leaders wanted me to do. But what were the alternatives? I didn't know. I wanted a course of action where I would be useful and the underlying purpose was meaningful—after all, I kept reminding myself, if I overlooked these objectives, what was the purpose of my life being saved? I concluded, for the time being, I would take a job—any job—and give myself more time to sort things out.

As I continued to mull over my future I found I kept coming back to my escape from the Holocaust horrors that had befallen family, friends, and millions of people I didn't even know—but not me. I lived while so many of my own relatives whom I loved, parents and their children of my age, perished. Why? What should be my response to the central event of my young life—being spared a terrifying death? I contemplated how to integrate the meaning behind being saved into a purposeful life. The lingering question demanded an answer. At this time my study of social ethics at Union started to become a dominant influence in my thinking. Joining the quest and struggle for social justice gradually evolved as my response to that question that haunted me, and I became committed to activism in different professional guises.

Me as a young boy.

My mother, Alice.

My father, Benno.

My parents on their wedding day.

My brother, Frank (right), and a fellow officer.

Aunt Malva

Aunt Vala

Uncle Boleslav and Aunt Mila

Aunt Julia

Uncle Paul

Me and Carolyn

Me and Paula

My speech at Moravian College

Paula

Chapter Nine: Being a Businessman and an Activist, 1952–1963

———————◆———————

O N THE FIRST day of my job search I expected to launch into a
series of inquiries over a number of days, or a week or so, before
I started working and drawing a salary. As it turned out, I was offered a
position right away as assistant to the owners of a small company that
manufactured lighting fixtures in New York City on East 22nd Street—
Neo-Ray Products. I took the job at fifty dollars per week. Inside of two
years I doubled my salary, which, of course, gave me a solid sense of
accomplishment—so much so that I began to consider the possibility
that business was the best fit for me as a vocational choice. However, the
Moravian Church ecclesiastical authorities did not share my enthusiasm
for a life committed to such pursuits. The church, I was reminded, had
invested in my education and it was payback time—either be ordained
and go into the ministry or start returning the college and seminary
loans. I chose the latter option and remained in business for the next
eleven years.

Three years later I moved to a larger manufacturer in the same field,
Litecraft Corporation, to take a more lucrative position. The job interview was unsettling to me. The interviewing vice president walked me
to a window overlooking the street, pointed to a shiny new bright-red
Cadillac convertible parked below and told me it belonged to the company president. "Wouldn't you love to have a car like that?" he sighed

longingly. He appeared almost to drool with envy and desire. The implication of the incident as I saw it was that he was dangling before me the possibility I too might secure such an over-priced toy—if I came to work for the company headed by the Cadillac owner. I mumbled an assenting phrase to answer the vice president's question while thinking that cars, even new shiny ones like the big boss's Cadillac, were not what I lusted after.

When I joined Litecraft its administrative offices were on East 36th Street. The location just off Fifth Avenue was an exciting one as it was within walking distance of many places that interested me, so I was disappointed when the company moved its offices to a new expanded manufacturing facility in Passaic, New Jersey. My responsibilities at Litecraft increased rapidly and I was promoted to assistant sales manager and corporate secretary. I began to travel to trade shows but quickly tired of being away from home. I worked every Saturday morning, which did not leave much time to pursue interests outside of the family. And something kept nagging at me. My discontent grew—not only with the hectic schedule required of my job; more importantly, I started feeling a betrayal of my personal pledge to pursue a life, which I was fortunate to have, striving for greater justice.

The growing civil rights movement, the Montgomery Alabama bus boycott, and the rising leadership of Dr. Martin Luther King made me realize I was contributing nothing to the values I supported and held most dear. I reminded myself that I needed to more actively pursue the ideals that defined me. I looked for opportunities, and in 1958, with several like-minded individuals, three of whom became close friends, we formed a Passaic County Chapter of Americans for Democratic Action. ADA was very involved with civil rights and related issues of social justice at both the state and federal levels, and Reinhold Niebuhr, whom I had greatly respected for years, was one of its founders and guiding lights. Within the organization I was elected cochair of our Passaic County Chapter as well as a member of the New Jersey state ADA Board. In 1962 I became state chairman. I was stimulated anew by events that included attending national ADA conventions in Washington, DC, coming into contact with Joe Rauh, Arthur Schlesinger, Hubert Humphrey, and others, and hosting Norman Thomas, the socialist candidate in many past presidential elections, when ADA invited him to be the featured speaker at the annual banquet. The following year I played the same role when Jimmy Roosevelt, the oldest son of Franklin Delano Roosevelt, was the ADA speaker. Yet something was still missing, and it was hard to identify what that was.

Carolyn and I bought a house in 1957 in New Jersey for our expanded family, which by then included two children. We decided upon a Christian upbringing for them, choosing St. John's Episcopal Church in Passaic, NJ. For me it was like coming home. Early memories of the village church I attended in England while living with Mother at Battle House during wartime flooded back. I felt I belonged there. Richard N. Bolles (later to author the successful book *What Color Is Your Parachute?*) was the rector of St. John's and integrated the parish by merging it with a black congregation, the only other Episcopal Church in town. But despite my leadership roles in ADA and participation in the life of St. John's, the quandary within me persisted—was this what my life was spared for? I couldn't yet answer in the affirmative. Would continuing to work in the lighting industry, which I recognized took more time as my responsibilities increased, distract me from ever carrying out purposeful goals to ultimately answer my nagging question? Was there more I should do beyond ADA and church activities? I decided I was not doing enough. Approaching my mid-thirties meant that in a few years I would be stuck professionally. Finally, I concluded I must devote myself full time to what I had decided mattered most to me—world peace efforts, working for social justice, and racial harmony.

But then I asked myself, what specifically was I qualified to do? Where would I fit in and how should I move beyond merely stating goals? There were two institutions I decided to examine—colleges and universities, and churches. Both I considered were dedicated in large measure to the pursuit of truth. I knew I could not leave my company immediately to tackle more years of expensive education since I was my family's sole provider. Without committing to years of study for a

PhD degree, I was not qualified for a long-term college or university teaching post. As I became more active at St. John's, I felt more a part of the Episcopal Church and interpreted this as a call to enter the ministry, for which I did have the requisite educational preparation.

Although I did not need additional seminary training, the Bishop of Newark felt I needed exposure to the "Episcopal ethos," so I enrolled as a special student for a year's study at General Theological Seminary in New York City. I lived at the seminary from Monday morning through Friday noon. My family managed without me during the week, and Carolyn obtained a position as organist and choir director at a Lutheran Church in Irvington, New Jersey. During this time we budgeted carefully in order to live off her salary and our savings.

At General Theological Seminary that year of 1963–64 I descended to the nadir of my adult life. I missed the family terribly. I made few friends and found the seminary inhospitable, focused on church trivia, and devoid of the social conscience I had expected. The high church atmosphere was unappealing, particularly chanting in the chapel, which was alien to my experiences thus far. I felt like the proverbial fish out of water but continued to push forward. While at General I did take the preliminary exam to be admitted as a graduate student and was able to complete the course work toward a master's degree although I did not finish my thesis for five years. My adviser would not approve any of the socially oriented subjects I proposed as research topics that reflected my, but not his, focus. I doggedly waited until he took a sabbatical leave, and was then assigned an interim adviser who was not so inflexible, and ultimately my thesis, *Taxation of Church Property,* was accepted. In it I argued that religious institutions should have their property taxed in order to not to be dependent on the state and thus, hopefully, regain their moral voice. I earned my master's degree in 1969. When my year of residency at General ended, I was extremely relieved. Now I was able to enter the next phase of my life's purpose full time—the ministry as a parish priest.

Chapter Ten: Being a Parish Priest and an Activist, 1964–1969

———————◆———————

IN JUNE OF 1964 my life took another turn when I began my career as a priest in the Episcopal Church. I felt ready to take on the challenges I knew would come. My first assignment as an Episcopal priest was at two small mission churches in New Jersey—Grace Episcopal Chapel in East Rutherford and St. Stephen's in the Delawanna section of Clifton. The combined average attendance at these churches was only about fifty people on a typical Sunday, which meant my parish duties were light and I had time to immerse myself in the struggle for racial equality and social justice raging in the country at that time. Because I believed Christian ethics demanded that churches support the civil rights movement, I joined with others to form a Newark Chapter of the Episcopal Society for Racial and Cultural Unity. The focus of ESCRU was primarily to improve race relations within the church, and our activities encompassed and addressed the current national debate. I volunteered to serve as one of the cochairs and was subsequently elected to the National Board of the organization. At that point I was convinced that entering the ministry was the right approach to ultimately determine an answer to the question that pursued and haunted me: for what purpose was I spared?

By mid-1960 the United States was in turmoil. The civil rights struggle, particularly in the South, was reaching a crescendo. In 1963 I participated in the March on Washington and, with others, was inspired by hearing Martin Luther King Jr.'s *I Have a Dream* speech. Things were moving quickly and the experiences were electrifying. In the nation's capital I looked across that vast sea of black and white faces and, in my idealism, felt that nothing could stop us now from pronouncing the end of racial bias and the savage actions that it engendered. But before long, more violence erupted with the use of attack dogs in Birmingham, Alabama, the imprisonment of Dr. King, the murder of civil rights activists Medgar Evers and Viola Liuzzo, and the Ku Klux Klan killings of three young men working to register African Americans to vote in Mississippi in 1964—James Chaney, Andrew Goodman, and Michael Schwerner.

The Newark Chapter of ESCRU concentrated on racial issues facing local churches and communities, the State of New Jersey, and the nation as a whole. The Sunday morning worship hour had been called the most segregated hour in America. We were encouraged that dialogue across racial lines, though it was not considered a significant step forward by many, was breaking new ground; and we hoped the communication would develop fresh understanding and trust. New relationships between some black and white people proved essential when racial unrest took off in New Jersey cities in 1967.

By the time the Newark riots began that year, protests were exploding in many American cities and increasingly turned violent. When the manhandling of demonstrators in Newark increased, ESCRU decided to station clergy, wearing our clerical collars, in police stations to try to minimize the brutality we heard was occurring there. I was among those dropped off at a police precinct in Newark where I was immediately confronted by a suspicious officer with, "What do you want here?"

"I just want to stay around and observe what is going on," I replied trying to use a non-confrontational voice.

"Why? What do you suspect?" he countered gruffly.

"We have learned about police brutality from some victims and we want to make sure nothing like that happens here." I tried to ignore his increasing irritation.

"You can stay if you like, but you won't see anything," he muttered, turning his back to me. He was clearly annoyed by my presence, and I was glad the confrontation was over. He was right—we saw nothing. In the booking room everything was orderly, but when the police took those arrested into a back room where we were not allowed to follow, we had no way of telling what happened. We learned from the experience to be more realistic in our planning, but symbolically it was an important show of solidarity with the black community. It was becoming clear to me how long and painful the struggle for racial harmony was going to be.

Another issue of growing importance and public concern was the US military expansion in Vietnam. Americans for Democratic Action continued to support the war and it led me to resign my membership and sever all contact. In its place, as the conflict in Vietnam escalated, I became active in the Clergy and Laity Concerned. The group was formed in 1965 by the National Council of Churches and was headquartered in New York City. The organization first became widely known in 1967 when it cosponsored a White House demonstration in conjunction with the Mobilization Committee to End the War in Vietnam. I made frequent trips to Washington, DC, during this time to demonstrate, meet with legislators, and attend conferences. Once I spearheaded a protest march in Hackensack, New Jersey, which led to my election as president of the Bergen County Council of Churches. Laypeople and clergy in the Newark diocese of the Episcopal Church who opposed the war proposed resolutions to end the conflict at their Annual Convention, and in 1968 I made a particularly impassioned appeal from the floor to pass such a resolution. I was moving further from my early profile in England as the shy, sometimes lonely "Czech Boy." I thought the meaning of my life had started to reveal itself. My objectives seemed more clear: to interpret, integrate, and now act in accordance with my convictions about human rights and world peace. But the declaration I chose to make before a large gathering at the 1968 Convention showed my discontent publicly, which later came "home to roost" with leaders of the denomination I was serving. In that short speech, I pleaded for the convention to support a resolution to end the unwarranted US interference in a civil war in Vietnam. Those remarks played a role in conferring upon me a new, more controversial image and taking me to another crossroad.

Based on my convictions about the Vietnam War, I was one of the plaintiffs in a lawsuit filed by the American Civil Liberties Union challenging the constitutionality of New Jersey sedition statute, N.J.Rev.Stat. § 2 A:148-22, which we argued had a chilling effect on the free expression of citizens' right to protest. We continued to demonstrate in the streets and won the case.

The effects of the war in Vietnam were brought directly home to me one evening when two marines came to the Vicarage and asked if I would accompany them to the home of an Episcopal family in town whom I did not know. I was told their son had been killed in action and the marines had to break this news to the parents; they wanted a clergyman with them. I felt compelled to go but could not find words of comfort that did not sound hollow in my attempt to assuage the grief brought on that family. The inability of either the representatives of the military or of the church to offer meaningful comfort was heartrending. The three of us did not prolong our stay, sensing that the parents needed to deal with their loss alone. For a long time afterward I pondered why, standing there next to the family, I became so inarticulate. All I could think is how terrible and unnecessary was the loss of those parents' son and the war itself; and the visit made a deep impression on me. I felt a kinship with them as I thought back to members of my own family and our friends and neighbors in Prague who perished or were forever changed as a result of the world war fought twenty-five years earlier.

But parish work also had its lighter moments. I was conscientious about calling on the shut-in, the sick and the elderly. One elderly man who suffered from emphysema lived on the top floor of a three-family house. I often climbed the long, rickety back staircase to visit him in the late afternoon. He was always glad to see me and talked nonstop to the point that I was required to say little or nothing. Several times I found myself nodding off. I was chagrined, but fortunately he took it with good humor.

I did enjoy preaching and frequently gave as illustrations events that currently stirred society and the world. I found writing sermons to be a creative form of self-expression and enjoyed developing a theme. As subjects for my texts I chose mainly the teachings and parables of Jesus and the condemnations by Old Testament prophets of the uncaring rich and powerful. One time when I was in the pulpit waxing eloquently about the misguided US policy in Vietnam, a man suddenly shot up out of his seat red-faced and huffed loudly for everyone to hear, "Bullshit!" He stared for a moment at me and the bewildered parishioners then walked slowly and deliberately down the aisle and left the church. I recovered and resumed my sermon before a congregation that sat in complete silence to the end. Later I visited the man when he was ill in the hospital, but neither of us mentioned the incident and he said he appreciated my visit.

The ministry had its surprises, too. A knock on our door one night revealed a tall, good-looking black man, just arrived from Trinidad, who had no place to live or even to sleep that night. Since the vicarage had a spare room in the attic, we offered it to him on a temporary basis. He gratefully accepted and stayed several days before making contact with friends in Brooklyn and left to accept their hospitality. Several months later, after I had lost touch with him, we saw him coming down the street with a large object hoisted on his shoulder. He proved to be an excellent cabinetmaker and had designed a gift he presented to us—a hanging wall desk using quality walnut to blend with our other furniture. This show of gratitude delighted the family, and we welcomed the useful piece he made for our home. His thoughtfulness was especially touching considering the small deed we thought we did for him in providing an unused room for a short time.

A later occupant of that room was Harry Moniba, a native of Liberia. He was a PhD candidate at New York University and needed a place to live while he made the short commute from East Rutherford to New York City to attend classes. At that time the Newark diocese had a close relationship with the Episcopal Church in Liberia, and I offered the attic room as a place to live for a Liberian student. Harry was born in

Bolahun, Liberia, where the Holy Cross Order, a Benedictine Anglican monastic community, had a mission with a school he attended. Harry was identified as a bright student and was brought to America to further his studies. His presence in our family for almost two years was exciting and heartwarming. He performed tricks with his "magic ring" and had us in stitches with imitations of TV and radio ads. Our kids loved Harry. He seldom ate with us, though, preferring to make his own food at about three o'clock in the morning when he finished studying. He had several close Liberian student friends and when they came to visit their infectious laughter could be heard throughout the neighborhood. I developed a life-long relationship with the Moniba family.

In the Episcopal Church the minister has discretion to use church buildings as he sees fit. The church in East Rutherford had a large free-standing parish hall, and I opened it to the larger community to hold dances for young people. Another use for the hall was as a voting location. One day I heard that an amateur theater company was denied a place to rehearse and perform because it wanted to produce a play called *The Tunnel of Love*. It was considered by some as too risqué. Since the parish hall was vacant and had a small stage, I offered the company the use of the hall, and the play was performed there. Thinking back, I wouldn't doubt that some of our own parishioners attended the mildly off-color play, but there were those in the community who disapproved. During the short run of the play I received several telephone calls from radio stations asking me for a comment about what prompted me to take such a "brave" stand. I was pleased that the episode was forgotten after the play closed. On another occasion I invited a peace march to use the sanctuary as a resting place. That decision, too, met with some opposition. One morning I found a Molotov cocktail on our front lawn, but luckily the fuse had gone out and it failed to explode. I took it to the police who were polite but clearly not interested. Discarded Molotov cocktails must have been a common find for them in those days of protest.

Four of us clergy members conducted many parish meetings and conferences about making the Church more relevant within contemporary society. I tried to apply our insights to the two small missions I was serving, both located near larger Episcopal parishes. I felt that it was poor use of scarce resources to keep these churches open for such a small group of people when they could easily attend other churches a short distance away. I sought to close the Delawanna Church, as its membership had declined to very few attendees. It had stayed in operation only with a significant subsidy from the diocese. I reasoned that the few parishioners could transfer to one of the nearby parishes. But at a parish meeting, the bishop, who seemed to support the plan earlier, changed his mind about closing the church. It appeared to me that he was more concerned about preserving property than focusing on how to allocate limited resources more effectively. I now understood how difficult it was for the Church to change both itself and respond to society. After this experience, my disillusion with the Church grew. A few years later the church in Delawanna was sensibly sold by the diocese and the parish was disbanded.

After five years at these two churches, I felt it was time to move on. I approached the bishop about a new assignment and was told candidly, "with your controversial image I can't place you anywhere." I let that sink in, then told myself that at least I knew where I stood; and at the end of 1968 I vowed that a year hence I would be elsewhere.

Again I faced my vocational choices as I thought about a new direction. I wondered where I belonged and how I should continue to shape the life I was saved to live. By May of 1969 I had received three distinctly different job offers. I could become the executive director of a social service center serving about one thousand families in the black community in Scranton, Pennsylvania. Or, I could be the assistant priest at Trinity Episcopal Cathedral in Newark, New Jersey, which had just merged with a mainly African and Caribbean American parish. The expanded cathedral congregation had recently chosen an African American dean to lead it, and he sought a white assistant who shared his views and values. My third option was to develop a new program at Trinity College in Hartford, Connecticut, to "build bridges" between the college and the community.

The location of the jobs, in Scranton, Newark, and Hartford, was not a primary consideration between the three positions for me, so location wasn't a deciding factor. The choice I needed to make depended on what type of institution was the best fit for me. Which one could I ascertain would be the most consistent agent for social change?

The position in Scranton appealed to me but there were drawbacks. I thought of a community center as ameliorating conditions rather than addressing systemic changes, which I was convinced were needed. A social service agency did not seem to me to be the most effective institution to work through. Also, I felt that a center serving the black community should have a black director and I pointed this out to the search committee. On these grounds I rejected the Scranton offer and was convinced I made the right decision.

The obstacle to the post at Trinity Cathedral in Newark was the institutional Church. I was disenchanted with the Church after my five years as parish priest. The disillusionment was over not only the Church's lack of commitment to social justice and peace but also its unwillingness to change its own structures. I made the decision to walk away from the Church and the parish ministry.

Although I had no experience with higher education since my student days, I regarded colleges and universities as the one institution that might be willing to exercise its influence to improve social conditions. I wondered later how I could have been so naive! But the challenge of working with students, several of whom participated in the interview process at Trinity College, appealed to me and I believed their actions could lead to promoting the cause of social justice that was so important to me. I chose the Trinity College option, and we moved to Hartford. My hopes were high that this newly created and largely undefined position would lead to the fulfillment I was seeking.

Chapter Eleven: Being an Educator and an Activist, 1969–1979

———————◆———————

DOES REPRESENTING AN educational institution of higher learning such as Trinity College justify using the term "educator" to describe oneself? I pondered this as I drove up the hill to the college on a pleasant August day in 1969. I was eager to bring my new position into clearer focus and expand the vague job description presented at my interview earlier that year. I walked by the impressive Trinity Chapel, constructed in Gothic style reminiscent of English churches I saw as a boy. I looked up at the traditional rose window and flanking towers with small stone ball-flowers attached like little noses and commonly used as a decorative motif on the towers and spires of monumental medieval cathedrals. Beyond the chapel was an expansive lush green lawn with well-chosen shade trees and a paved walkway leading to students' living areas, offices, and meeting halls. Architecturally, much of Trinity College recalls historic sites from the Middle Ages that I visited and was impressed by during my years in England. I remember as a youth gawking at the finely detailed stone carvings on my first visit to Lincoln Cathedral when I lived on the IVSP farm in Lincolnshire. This bucolic campus where I was now employed was built on the upper part of the hill and contrasted with pockets of deterioration that defined the Hartford neighborhoods situated at the lower elevations of the area. I wondered how one begins to create meaningful programs to link these two disparate settings. Mulling over the challenges ahead I found myself wondering, again, if I might be a fish out of water—the feeling I had earlier while preparing for the ministry.

The job I had accepted was as director of the Office of Community Affairs. One aspect of the newly created position immediately appealed to me: the college had given no specific expectations of what I should focus on. I interpreted this to mean I was to carve out and define my role myself; and, indeed, I was given the freedom and latitude to do so. My initial conversations with people on campus, in the nearby neighborhood, and in the larger city beyond, convinced me that there was a huge gulf between those who occupied the college grounds and people who lived on the other side of the tall fence that enclosed the academic bastion. The accepted interpretation of this physical separation seemed to be that there were two distinct worlds in that part of the city. I learned that most residents who lived and worked in the area around the campus had never been on Trinity's grounds even once. By the same token there were people on campus who avoided the neighborhood and thought it unnecessary for the college to be concerned with it.

A crucial question became how much was the college committed to change? The impetus for creating the office that I staffed came directly from a student action in April 1968, when a group of them locked up the trustees of the college and demanded that Trinity become more responsive to students and the needs of the city. Subsequently, the college applied for a grant to the Hartford Foundation for Public Giving to create my Office of Community Affairs. The official rationale for funding was to build bridges between Trinity College and Hartford and its residents, but not as obvious was the administration's desire to manage the students and channel their energy "more acceptably."

A test of the college's commitment came two years later when funds from the grant were about to expire and Trinity had to decide whether to discontinue the office or support it with its own funds. I had accepted the position with full knowledge that nothing was assured beyond two years, but despite the lack of job security we decided to buy a house in the integrated Blue Hills neighborhood of Hartford.

Our decision to locate in Blue Hills was influenced by a contact at Trinity who lived in Blue Hills and our attorney, the state representative for that area. Soon after we moved, Blue Hills began experiencing a major demographic change, and neighborhood issues moved to center stage. The largely Jewish population in the area was aging, and many long-time residents were moving out. Young black families began to move in. The realtors, hoping for quick profits, tried to induce panic selling among non-black homeowners, but many residents responded by putting signs on their lawns stating "We won't sell." They were courageously committed to keeping their neighborhood integrated.

I was elected to the board of the Blue Hills Civic Association (BHCA) shortly after we moved in. The Association proved to be an entrée for me to meet Hartford's political and community leaders. In 1969 Hartford experienced the last of four consecutive summers of racial unrest. The board of the BHCA met with the city manager, the chief of police, and leaders of the black community to discuss police brutality, as it had become a major issue and remained at the forefront of discussions for the next three decades.

By 1972 through 1974, the Blue Hills neighborhood was rapidly tipping to majority black ownership. The BHCA spun off a subsidiary called the Blue Hills Housing Services Corporation and I served on its board as well. We tried various ways to keep the neighborhood biracial, even creating a bumper sticker designed to attract suburban commuters that said "Blue Hills Commuters Don't!" since Blue Hills residents did not have to commute—already being in the city. But nothing could stop the white exodus, and by the mid-1970s Blue Hills was predominantly an African American area.

Carolyn was also active in the community. She was elected PTA president for the Annie Fisher School, which all three of our children attended. She also became the organist at the Horace Bushnell Congregational Church in Hartford, which had just welcomed a new, dynamic pastor. Our whole family joined this congregation, which was committed to maintain its interracial membership by embracing both neighborhood and suburban residents. A social action committee was formed at the church, and that became another forum for me to address community issues and act upon my convictions. Once, to mark our solidarity with victims of police brutality, members of the committee carried a coffin draped in black down a main avenue to City Hall and left it at the entrance to visually illustrate our message.

These activities in which I took leadership roles led to my increased visibility and resulted in my nomination by the mayor in 1974 to the city's Human Relations Commission. I served on the commission for more than twenty years, several years as chairman. The Human Relations Commission's mission is to act to improve racial and social conditions and advocate for economic justice for all Hartford residents. Serving on the commission provided an excellent vantage point from which to observe and sometimes influence city politics and policies. Police brutality was not the only issue on the commission's plate. We dealt with discrimination in housing, employment, education, and other situations as they arose—all issues that I cared about and wanted to help address.

While Carolyn was the organist at Horace Bushnell Church, a young black man, new to the area from Baltimore, went to speak with her one Sunday. "Could I sing in your choir?" he asked her. Never one to turn down someone who wants to sing, she welcomed him and so began our lifelong friendship with James R. Reed Jr., and later with his family. Jim and I worked together on many social justice issues. Recording the details of his life would fill another memoir, but suffice it to say that he and his bride prepared for their wedding ceremony from our house, and later we celebrated together the births of each of their five children and hailed subsequent successes. Jim and I have supported each other during the ups and downs of life.

In summertime I sometimes filled in for vacationing ministers. These substituting jobs helped the churches and supplemented my income. I enjoyed the variety, but sometimes when I was at the altar, I heard an inner voice—*What's a "nice Jewish boy" like you doing here?* The messages reminded me of unwanted pop-up ads. When later I formally resigned from the ministry, the voice died away.

At Trinity College I began to work closely with students. While those in the Students for a Democratic Society showed disdain for me as a tool of the administration, there was another more supportive group that organized as Trinity College Action Center (TCAC). In discussions among students, faculty, and administration, we concluded that the most lasting changes would come only through impacting Trinity's institutional structures. Two changes led the way. To begin with, women were admitted for the first time starting in the fall term of 1969. I noted from the outset that women were more interested than men in all types of community service. Secondly, a new curriculum went into effect that fall. Many course requirements were reexamined and some were eliminated. In addition, students became able to design their own studies for credit under a faculty member's direction and approval.

I was excited about the changes. The more flexible curriculum gave me an opportunity to develop internships in the community where the quid pro quo was the student's contribution to an agency that had been evaluated for quality and commitment; and, on the other side, achievement outcomes by the student of defined learning objectives derived from the experience. Each internship required a faculty sponsor. At first I was able to identify only a few faculty members willing to supervise independent studies, which included a field placement, but that changed as internships became more accepted. I first developed the program by identifying suitable field placements and then published a handbook that described internship opportunities available primarily in social agencies, in schools, and in government. The initial step was to interest students and convince a faculty member that there was academic merit in field learning. I liked working with students to develop internships, knowing that we were building a worthwhile program that hopefully would continue into the future. And, indeed, over the years the number of students in internships has grown at Trinity College so that there is now a permanent multi-staffed office to help students find suitable placements.

A further objective of TCAC was to create an interdisciplinary program in Urban Studies that would provide an academic focus on the city. After two years of work, the Urban Studies Program became a reality and an economist was chosen as director. Shepherding the proposal through the college's curriculum committee gave me insight into how colleges work, and this was a much-needed learning experience for me. From a modest beginning, the Urban Studies Program blossomed into a full-fledged Center of Urban and Global Studies, and I felt rather like a feathered father pleased with his fledgling that was starting to function on its own.

Another role Trinity played vis-à-vis the city was to provide a much-needed meeting space. The campus was viewed as neutral turf, which proved very useful in arranging citywide meetings and conferences. The community forums on education my office sponsored in the early 1970s are an example. These gatherings held on Saturday mornings featured nationally recognized speakers followed by small discussion groups led by Trinity faculty members. Educators, parents, and residents from all parts of the city attended.

From the community forums on education that I started was formed an alternative high school named Shanti School, a placement choice for students unable to cope with a formal curriculum in a large setting. I recall several Irish colleagues who worked with me as effective community organizers and in education positions where they were caring and sensitive—and, like Gene Mulcahy, they were great fun. I was a board member of Shanti and Gene served as principal. Once when Gene and I were scheduled to meet with an executive of a large downtown department store in Hartford, we brought along one of our students, Theresa, a dark-skinned, well-built senior. On the way back down the escalator we passed the bridal shop and Gene had a sudden idea. He gave us roles to play—Theresa was the bride-to-be, I was her father, and Gene took the part of the prospective groom. We told the saleslady we were looking for just the right wedding gown for Theresa, the implication being money was no object. I hovered over Theresa telling her, "Pick anything you like, dear, nothing is too good for you." As I warmed to my persona I added comments like, "Take your time, remember this is going to be the special day you've always dreamed of." Theresa inspected several gowns, cooing appropriately, while Gene hovered close by nodding approval now and then. We were able to stay in character for about fifteen minutes but finally, still pretending to be shoppers, left disgruntled, taking the escalator to the main floor where we burst into uncontrollable laughter. We all felt a bit sorry for the saleslady, but at least we had provided her with dinner conversation that evening.

I remember Gene as not only irrepressible and spontaneous, but also as a brilliant and dedicated educator. On another occasion, Gene, along with a teacher in the school, visited me at home in full academic regalia and with great flourish presented an "honorary" diploma that bestowed on me all the rights and privileges of a Shanti School graduate. Gene left Shanti in 1980, and the school closed shortly thereafter.

Other Trinity College facilities were largely unused during the summer months, so I offered them for community use. The college's athletic center became home for a city-funded recreation summer program and later also the NCAA National Youth Sports Program. A professional repertory company was formed with my assistance and support at the Austin Arts Center and performed under the name Summerstage for several seasons. The Trinity College Chapel became the venue for a summer chamber music series to precede the established Wednesday evening carillon concerts. All these efforts strengthened the bond between the college and the community. I was busier than ever engaged in these and other projects.

As funds from the Hartford Foundation for Public Giving were about to expire in the spring of 1971, I had anxious moments but survived the crisis. After much vacillation, the college finally decided to make the Office of Community Affairs and my position a permanent one, without foundation support. That commitment lasted only four years. Facing financial pressures, Trinity decided to transfer me to another post and made me the director of Graduate Studies with the understanding I should continue all my community activities. It was an odd arrangement. I was now to report to the dean of the faculty. My one lasting contribution to the graduate program was to help create a master's degree program in Public Policy, a cooperative venture between Trinity College and the University Of Connecticut School Of Law.

When Carolyn and I moved from our house into a condo, I began to notice the blank wall opposite my computer in the new study I had set up. How to decorate it? Then it struck me, why not mount some of the plaques, certificates, and awards presented to me over the years? These citations on the wall would represent for me a summary of my working life and as a group remind me of the struggles to achieve past goals. On the few occasions when I take note of these mementos, they bring to mind accomplishments I feel most proud of.

Yet it occurs to me now that what I consider my most significant achievement at Trinity College doesn't show up on that wall at all. This was working with a federally funded program called Upward Bound, designed to help high school students, and bringing it to the campus. The purpose of Upward Bound appealed to me the moment I heard about it. As a national program, it was designed to prepare low-income, at-risk high school students for entry into and successful completion of a post-secondary education they otherwise would most certainly have been denied. I recall long working sessions alone that took me away from many holiday activities during the 1971 Christmas break. But the outcome of my researching and writing a grant proposal enabled the college to undertake an Upward Bound program. I turned to state elected officials to secure their support in advocating for the proposal. The program consisted of a six-week summer residency on campus with students attending small classes led by experienced teachers. I especially liked the provision that continued academic support for the students throughout the school year. Working with the overseeing board, we selected a young African American man to be the first director, but unfortunately he had to be terminated two years later on grounds of sexual malfeasance. Trouble ensued. The man hired a white lawyer to contest the firing decision, and at a community meeting I was accused of being a racist—definitely a new and unhappy first for me! But the board supported me and the outcome was positive.

After that turmoil subsided, the next two directors of Upward Bound, both representing minorities, led the program successfully for twenty more years until the Federal Department of Education ceased its funding. But the legacy of this farsighted program remains significant. One need only look at the twelve hundred Hartford participants who enrolled in the program, 70 percent of whom graduated from college. As adults one became the police chief in Hartford, one the mayor of the city, and one was elected Connecticut's state treasurer. Other graduates of Upward Bound left their marks by assuming a wide variety of leadership roles. When I left Trinity, the Upward Bound director started reporting to the dean of the faculty, and it pleased me that the position was now fully integrated into the structure of the college.

I continued my involvement with the Frog Hollow neighborhood immediately adjacent to Trinity's campus. In 1975 the Roman Catholic diocese brought in professionally trained community organizers who began to meet with residents and organize them into block clubs. The members of these block clubs then went to City Hall to demand improvements to their neighborhood, such as better garbage collection, eradication of rats, and cleaner streets.

I welcomed the opportunity to work with grassroots neighborhood residents within the new organization called Hartford Areas Rally Together (HART). A memorable moment occurred when the lead organizer came to a meeting with college officials and declared proudly, "I now have you surrounded with block clubs." What he meant was that on many blocks around campus there were groups of people from that block who met regularly to discuss the needs of the area and how to deal with them. A fruitful dialogue started.

With HART's assistance and a group of neighborhood businessmen, I was instrumental in forming a real estate development company to address the housing deterioration in the Frog Hollow neighborhood. At the same time, a report issued by the Greater Hartford Process, a business-funded planning agency, recommended the three major institutions in the South End of Hartford—Trinity College, Hartford

Hospital, and the Institute of Living, a mental health institution—play a more active role in improving the neighborhoods around them.

These developments, underscored by the continuing deterioration of the Frog Hollow neighborhood, provided me the context for proposing that Trinity College form a coalition with its next-door healthcare institutions—Hartford Hospital and the Institute of Living. Trinity's president, Theodore Lockwood, took the lead in presenting the idea to these institutions; and by 1978 the Southside Institutions Neighborhood Alliance (SINA) was formed, incorporated, and hired its first director, Robert Pawlowski, on a part-time basis. I had met Bob a few years earlier when he was a young social studies teacher at Northwest Catholic High School in West Hartford and with a group of his urban studies students researched the underclasses of Hartford and published their findings in *How the Other Half Live.* I was very impressed and recognized Bob as an up-and-coming personality. I was the Trinity representative on the board of SINA, and when Bob left in 1979 to pursue other ventures I was asked to become its full-time director. I accepted eagerly.

My early assumption which led me to Trinity College in the first place was that colleges and universities were altruistic institutions. I learned, however, that self-interest is a major factor in institutional decisions. Trinity College's commitment to its surrounding neighborhoods grew and in response to continued pressure from neighborhood residents and city leaders, the college administration acknowledged that community involvement benefited it as well. I felt a sense of accomplishment as I ended my first decade at Trinity. I was ready for a transition to head a new organization, SINA, with a broader institutional base but still addressing the same problems and challenges.

Chapter Twelve: Being a President and an
Activist, 1979–1999

———————◆———————

I HAD ARRIVED! At the Southside Institutions Neighborhood Alliance
I attained a distinguished new title—president and CEO. Granted,
the nonprofit corporation I would head had but *two* employees, my secretary and myself, but at SINA I had a broader mandate to represent
three major institutions rather than just one. My focus also expanded
to include citywide activities. I relished being involved in new spheres,
and I often registered amazement at being paid for work that directly
reflected what I believed in—working to improve conditions for people
in the neighborhood, standing up for civil rights, and guarding against
police brutality while supporting better policing of the area. My work
seemed to be leading, finally, to authentic fulfillment; my accomplishments would serve a purpose and have meaning outside of my immediate circle and beyond myself.

In the SINA position I became involved in multiple new challenges
that did not always work out as I hoped. In the early 1980s the Linkage
Project in Hartford sought to channel a portion of the profits from the
booming downtown development to a fund to improve the neighborhoods. I supported the project's goals, but the efforts of this all-inclusive
coalition of neighborhood representatives, the business community, and
the city failed when support from the Chamber of Commerce was withdrawn. The failure to create this linkage was disappointing, but a few

years later many of the same people formed the Hartford Vision Project to achieve similar goals. Unfortunately, this effort was also doomed to failure when the business sector withdrew and the comprehensive final report, for which I played a significant role, was shelved like so many other studies.

There were also developments emerging across the country that were engaging to me. In 1980 the Nuclear Freeze movement began and quickly started a national push for nuclear disarmament. It was an issue I had actively supported since the mid-1950s, and I became immersed in it—organizing a strong Connecticut contingent to participate in the 1982 rally in New York City at the United Nations, which brought more than a million people together. But the animosity of those opposed became evident as we marched through the streets where we were showered by missiles, some containing human feces.

During the 1984 presidential election season, I experienced political power firsthand. As a result of a hard-fought battle in the caucus of the First Congressional District, I was elected a delegate to the Democratic Convention in San Francisco supporting the candidacy of Gary Hart, a Yale graduate and US Senator from Colorado. At the caucus it was determined that the Hart delegation was entitled to one more delegate. As the leader of the Hart delegation, it fell to me to select the person. I recall standing in the hallway surrounded by several potential delegates, all of whom wanted to be the one chosen. For the first time ever, I felt the rush of adrenalin and power—this was up to me. I knew I would make enemies of those I rejected and would curry favor with the person I named. The situation had the kind of peril that politicians dealt with all the time and it filled me with a strange exhilaration. Finally I put all trepidation aside and made the choice then and there.

The Connecticut delegation was led by Governor William O'Neill and the Hart delegates were assigned rows of seats in back of the majority Walter Mondale supporters. When our candidate was nominated, we erupted with appropriate volume. Sitting immediately in front of me was another Hart delegate, Kingman Brewster, a former president of Yale. When he began waving his Hart banner vigorously and shouting,

I overrode my reserved tendencies and said to myself, "If Kingman Brewster can make a fool of himself, so can I!" I found it satisfying to let off steam even though we realized that the establishment candidate would be nominated and our effort would fall short.

In addition to being involved in these citywide and national issues, I began to put more effort into upgrading the worsening conditions in the Frog Hollow neighborhood of Hartford. SINA's mission was to improve the neighborhoods surrounding the three member institutions. The objective was to provide a better, safer environment in which these entities might flourish. There was no more urgent place to begin than in Frog Hollow. The SINA board and I started formulating plans but decided on two key steps to accomplish before we went further. First, the community needed its own voice, so we assisted in starting a community newspaper called the *Southside News* (renamed later the *Hartford News)*. We recognized that launching a newspaper was risky business, and the success of the venture rested with Robert Pawlowski, SINA's previous part-time director, who had become the newspaper's publisher and editor. In his memoir, *Something in Common,* Bob summarizes the challenges we faced in those early days:

> Before we actually started taking on the financial burden of the editor's salary and the printing, typesetting and layout expenses that were staring us in the face, we had to get a little money. We needed at least enough for two issues, we thought. We then would have enough advertisers—or Ivan would figure something out—we were sure. He did convince SINA to put up $2,500 "seed money" and we figured that kind of left him on the hook for more if we got short further down the line. Then there was the challenge of selling ads.

SINA did put up a little more money, but in very short order *Southside News* was on its own.

The second need was to address the physical condition of the Frog Hollow neighborhood, which was riddled with closed stores and abandoned buildings. In cooperation with HART, the community organization, and a group of Park Street businessmen, SINA helped found a nonprofit real estate development corporation named Broad Park Development Corporation or simply Broad Park. This was an important step. I became a board member and stayed on the board for more than twenty years, relying on Broad Park as the primary vehicle through which SINA addressed the neighborhood's housing and commercial development needs. One of our major achievements was building an enclosed market called El Mercado that housed several merchants and became one of the hubs of the Puerto Rican community. Broad Park also renovated and managed almost five hundred units of low income housing, and its success continued despite many vicissitudes along the way.

I participated in several efforts to upgrade Park Street, the commercial spine of the neighborhood. I met frequently with business representatives to discuss improvements—better lighting, repaired sidewalks, more available parking, more attractive store facades, and increased safety. We were disappointed that none of these plans came to fruition, and I was learning how hard it was to raise money for poor neighborhoods. Disappointments were frequent, but I could not let my personal feelings slow down the work I set out to do. Eventually we were successful in obtaining funding from the Federal Streetscape Improvement Incentive Program to complete the project.

The relationship between HART and me oscillated between cooperative and adversarial, depending largely upon who staffed HART. One of HART's troubling techniques was applied at annual congresses to which city officials and other leaders, including me, were invited. In the proceedings we were asked about our commitments, but no details or explanations could be voiced as HART allowed only a curt "yes" or "no" answer. It was my view that when HART found it convenient to depict SINA as the "bad guys" they did so, but at other times they would treat us as useful allies. Relations with HART improved markedly in the early 1990s when SINA began to fund an organizer who worked for HART.

Education, especially the preparation of students in elementary and secondary schools, was particularly important to all three SINA institutions, and I spent much time discussing and planning with leaders how to address this issue. Trinity College wanted well-prepared students, and the two hospitals needed competent employees to hire and train. In the early 1980s, SINA began to design and implement some programs. Early on, a successful partnership with the Betances Elementary School, which had a particularly dynamic principal, was formed.

An educational program titled Scholar of the Month was initiated and proved quite successful. It started with an idea proposed by a SINA board member that I was able to develop into a program. Actualizing an idea and making it workable is something I did well and enjoyed doing. The intent was to recognize local academically achieving high school students; we'd select them based solely on their grade-point average since no other award program centered entirely on academics. Eight students were chosen, one each month from October through May, from each of the four high schools in the city, including a Catholic high school, for a total of thirty-two students each year. The students and their parents were honored at a banquet at the end of the school year where I got to meet and congratulate the chosen students.

Building on that experience, SINA began a special relationship with a large high school which serves SINA's target neighborhoods. We chose and paid for one of its teachers to be SINA's representative to recruit students to visit SINA institutions, to set up shadowing opportunities for students with professionals and learn what they do, to participate in tutoring and mentoring, and to provide a course on study techniques. After several years, we decided to expand the program and sponsor college scholarships each year at Bulkeley High School for three students based upon their community service. Stipends were one thousand dollars for each of the four years in college. After I retired, to my great surprise and delight, SINA named this program Ivan A. Backer Scholarships.

All of these educational efforts culminated in the development of The Learning Corridor, which SINA later spearheaded. An entire one-block site between the campuses of the Institute of Living and Trinity College had been a trolley barn in the early part of the twentieth century and later became a garage for buses. The noise, traffic, and air pollution were a source of great annoyance and disruption to neighboring residents, who started to agitate for the removal of the bus garage in the mid-1980s. The fact that the facility had grown too small for the larger fleet of buses meant the buses that could not be housed inside had to be parked outside with their engines running all night during the winter. HART and SINA supported the push to have the garage moved. We succeeded in convincing our congressional representative, Barbara Kennelly, to obtain federal funding for a new bus garage in a more appropriate area some miles away, which was completed in 1991.

The question of what should happen to the abandoned bus property was hotly debated. In light of the housing shortage at the time, plans were originally drawn up for low density, owner-occupied housing. But first the severely polluted land had to be cleaned up. Waste of all kinds had been dumped on the ground from the trolley depot days, and after the conversion to a bus center waste oil was poured out to add to the already polluted earth. The State of Connecticut, which owned the property, eventually appropriated six million dollars to clean up the site. However, by the mid-1990s the housing crisis had eased and a new vision was put forth—to group several schools onto the large site. When the project was completed in 1996 it was named The Learning Corridor and became home to an elementary Montessori School, a magnate middle school, the Greater Hartford Academy for the Arts, and the Greater Hartford Academy of Mathematics and Science—all of them serving students from both Hartford and the suburbs.

Whatever SINA accomplished in the seventeen years I led it was due in equal part to an active and very supportive board of directors made up of two representatives from each of the three-member institutions. Later, membership was increased to include two then neighboring institutions—Connecticut Children's Medical Center and Connecticut Public Television, and I headed a five-member organization.

This last part of my career, which involved other assignments where I needed to develop, organize, and manage programs and projects designed to help people in the Hartford community, is summarized below by Bob Pawlowski in his memoir, cited earlier. I am touched whenever I read it.

> *Ivan Backer contributed in some way to almost every Hartford venture I got involved in for more than three decades. I don't know why this was. Personally, we had little in common. He was one of the few people I knew who devoted his life to things he believed—mainly civil rights. I always told people that Ivan did things and got things accomplished because he believed. Most often he had little money and no power, but that never stopped him. He was relentless and would attend meeting after meeting after meeting to achieve the smallest of things. Other people I knew called him a missionary. I guess that was true.*

I had finally developed the meaningful career I sought after those years of casting about and met goals I once feared were unachievable. Now I considered retirement. When I turned sixty-five, I reviewed the retirement benefits to which I was entitled and realized that we could manage with my pension and Social Security. The stock market boom helped immensely. I was tired of the constant round of evening meetings and felt some discouragement that weighed on me about the slowness of achieving results, the bureaucratic difficulties that had to be overcome with each project or new idea, and the small incremental steps that realistically could be expected. I was starting to burn out. I signaled to the Board that I would retire by the middle of 1995, although that period was prolonged until the end of the following year because a successor had not been found in time.

I was honored at two retirement parties. The first, in the neighborhood at a local bar owned by Bob Pawlowski and a couple of his friends, is best described by him:

> *When Ivan retired in 1996, we had a roast for him at Camila's that included a dance by the Ivanettes, female impersonators organized by our resident "wise guys" who were big fans of Ivan. ... The Ivanettes all wore polyester suits hunted down at Goodwill. Not to be outdone,*

Ivan, who somehow got wind of the spoof, appeared through the back door dressed in a cowboy outfit. Father Dave MacDonald, a Jesuit priest and one of the co-founders of HART and often one of Ivan's co-conspirators, was the major roaster. Listening to his no-holds-barred delivery, you would never have known he was a priest—or one of Ivan's strongest allies in making good things happen for Hartford people.

I will never forget that evening as I entered Camila's. My crack of the rented whip commanded respect. A ten-gallon hat, cowboy boots, and a stick horse completed my outfit. The party was a howl! The more constrained official event, held at Hartford Hospital, was lavish, and had more people and a parting gift that made me do a double-take—a trip for Carolyn and me to a destination of our choice. A year later we fulfilled a long-held dream by going on an educational trip to Greece and Turkey.

I continued with SINA in a consulting capacity for four years, managing all the educational programs as well as the Neighborhood Service Award through which SINA recognized five outstanding people who worked to benefit the neighborhoods either as volunteers or professionals. The decision to move gradually into retirement by working part-time was a good one. It made for a smooth transition at SINA and allowed me to let go gradually. But by the end of 1999, I was ready to cut the tie and start the new millennium fully retired.

Chapter Thirteen: Being Retired and Still an Activist, 1999–Now

———————◆———————

MORE TIME TO follow world events was what I looked forward to as one retirement benefit. In August 2001, less than a month before the 9/11 attacks, I put down the *New York Times* I had been reading and said to Carolyn, "You know, it can't continue like this forever without repercussions." I had in mind the great and growing gap between us in America who were prospering and those elsewhere in the world who were living in poverty. I agreed with those who criticized a growing American arrogance toward other nations, our careless use of precious world resources—water, fossil fuels, timber, open land—our exploitation of cheap overseas labor, and our disregard for how entire ecosystems were being endangered. I ended my rant with, "Something has to give. I'm afraid we'll get our comeuppance if we continue this way."

Little did I realize that in a few weeks it would happen. I had basked in retirement activities for over a year and was home that morning coping with the frustration of trying to log on to the *New York Times* website and finding I could not. I knew why after a friend called who was watching television—the *Times* was inundated with people wanting to read the latest reports on attacks by air on American targets—something most Americans never considered possible. The date was September 11, 2001.

I got to the TV in time to see footage of smoke clouds billowing from one of the World Trade Center towers in New York City. The camera suddenly switched to show a plane aimed straight at the second tower, which exploded into a fireball on impact. A little later the first tower tumbled down upon itself as if it were a sand castle demolished by the tide. I could not believe what I was seeing. There would be thousands of victims. As I stared at the screen to get more details, I marveled at the precision of such a concerted and unprecedented attack not only on the Trade Center towers but, the voice rumbled on, the Pentagon as well. Suddenly another airborne attack attempt was disclosed. This fourth was foiled but obviously it was aimed at some other crucial target. When my shock subsided a bit, I speculated about the rage that must have motivated those suicide-driven murderers. Then it hit me that a short time before I had predicted America would experience its comeuppance—and here it was right in front of me.

I shuddered when the president declared a War on Terror. It is impossible to extinguish a concept by military force, I thought. But most Americans seemed to be going along even when the administration in 2003 didn't hesitate to invade Iraq, without provocation. I felt helpless and depressed, unable to join the street protests since I was recovering from triple bypass heart surgery. I anxiously watched TV while exercising in rehab, lamenting every military strike and the growing number of casualties. I was still an activist, though certainly more of an inactive one in my recovery period.

Before my surgery I resigned from a number of boards of directors, selecting to continue on two which supported important social and physical improvements in Hartford. I also resigned from the City of Hartford Human Relations Commission, on which I had served for more than two decades. I needed to slow down.

To my immense surprise while recuperating that spring I was contacted by my alma mater, Moravian College, and informed that I had been chosen as recipient of the Haupert Humanitarian Award, named after Raymond Haupert, who was president of the college when I was enrolled as an undergraduate. As mentioned earlier, one of the jobs I was happy to have in those college years of scarce resources was doing outside chores, often beside President Haupert himself, in the extensive gardens at his residence. I don't recall when I became aware of the existence of the award named for President Haupert. The award is a selective tribute and not given every year. Receiving this humanitarian award is the most gratifying acknowledgment I have ever received relating to my activism.

I was informed there would be a ceremony in October, at which I was asked to give an acceptance speech. Carolyn was looking forward to returning to Behlehem, the city of her birth, to see me so honored. But Carolyn died that summer unexpectedly in Yosemite Park, where we were vacationing. She had been diagnosed with heart disease years earlier, but was feeling well throughout our trip. One of the most difficult tasks I faced was calling each of my three children to tell them of their mother's death. In the fall my two daughters accompanied me to the event. I was presented with a glass bowl etched with the college emblem and mounted on a jet black stand with a silver plate inscription. I display the bowl prominently in my living room. The purpose of the award is "to honor an alumna or alumnus who has rendered outstanding service in the cause of human welfare. The Alumni Association is honored to present the 2003 Haupert Humanitarian Award to Ivan Backer '49 in recognition of his leadership in community revitalization."

The remarks I made on that occasion were in a sense my valedictory:

I have been very lucky in life because I was paid for what I wanted to do. I was able to live out my values, to work for causes I believed in, and make a living at it. Unfortunately, not many people can say that. And I found and developed some of these values here at Moravian. ... When I began my work in Hartford in 1969, I felt that as a society we were going to make some headway in the struggle against racism, sexism, poverty, and injustice. For a long time that sense of purpose sustained me, as I and others slowly chipped away at these problems.

But today, some fifty plus years after leaving Moravian, I am far less sanguine. Poverty, injustice, entrenched privilege seem to be more intractable. The gap between the haves and the have-nots is widening within the United States but even more significantly between the first and third worlds. While we in America can spend thousands of dollars per person to get or to stay healthy, some of the world's children can't even get shots to prevent them from catching measles.

I fear for this country. Today, we in the US are too comfortable, too complacent, and too self-centered and arrogant. And I think that if we do not change, if we do not commit ourselves to bettering our society, to building a more equitable world community, and to helping struggling countries across the globe, that things will turn out badly for us.

Returning to Hartford a new activity grabbed my attention. It is called the Adult Learning Program (ALP). ALP is a member of the Network of Learning Institutes in Retirement, sponsored by Road Scholar/ Elderhostel and under the auspices of the University of Connecticut. ALP opened its doors for retired local residents to share their love of learning. In addition to being able to take courses, participants also have the opportunity to teach a course or lead a session. ALP supplements its own resources by inviting community leaders and professors from surrounding colleges and universities to share their knowledge with us. The enrollment fee is minimal. A few other adult education groups have been organized in Hartford and some area communities, but their close connection with a designated college or university that pays speakers to give courses makes those programs too costly for many retired adults who do not have extra income at their disposal.

I wanted to delve into areas of knowledge I had neglected during my years of full-time employment. My parents and many adult relatives were lifelong learners and I wanted that influence to be a greater part of my retirement life. Looking back I recognized how important educational opportunity was in my young life and later in choosing what to emphasize in my community work. ALP was a logical next step for me.

I was energized by the Adult Learning Program and quickly found myself up to my eyeballs in obligations—attending classes, facilitating courses, serving on the ALP Curriculum Committee, and becoming a member of the ALP Advisory Board. I was able to rekindle contacts from past years to help us carry out ALP goals. As in my educator days, I didn't really think of myself as a teacher, but I wanted to participate to make the ALP programs work for those who were joining in greater numbers. I was comfortable volunteering as a discussion leader and eventually a cochair of the organization. Again I felt an activist.

For ALP I led trips to the capital city of Hartford, reported on sessions of the Hartford City Charter Revision, and talked about nuclear disarmament and other past and current history topics. I presented some slide shows and travel talks about our overseas trips. I took a variety of interesting ALP courses myself and became one of a growing number of learners under our umbrella—poetry, short stories, play reading, history, and creative writing became my favorite topics. Retirement activities were like a feast laid before me from which I could make selections. Here was my opportunity to delve deeply into the arts and use the creative part of my brain. Carolyn joined me in some of these courses and offered her own in music.

Included among my new interests was a greater appreciation of film. When I heard in 2010 that Cinestudio, an independent film theater on the campus of Trinity College, would likely be forced to close its doors because it did not have the funds to purchase new digital projection equipment, I was spurred into action. Not only did Cinestudio show movies not screened elsewhere in Greater Hartford, but the theater was important to me as a vital link to the community to which I had dedicated so many years already. In response I led a successful fund-raising effort to purchase the needed equipment.

I had been a president and board member of the Knox Foundation for years, a foundation that uniquely spent its endowment to jump-start the rejuvenation of Hartford's downtown. When my term on the board expired, I was still very concerned about some of the foundation's priorities—the poor public transit system in the Greater Hartford area, the increasing congestion on the highways, and the spread of sprawl due to lack of land-use planning. A number of us from Knox joined with others to form a new organization in 1998 that would focus on transportation and land use. Specifically, we advocated for a light rail connection from Hartford to Bradley Airport. We called ourselves All Aboard! and spent many hours building a strong citizen organization of nearly one thousand members and advocating for a more coherent and balanced transportation system. I decided to remain on the board and executive committee and headed up the fund-raising. All Aboard! merged with One Thousand Friends of Connecticut, a state-wide organization with similar goals, in 2008.

In retirement I also began to more actively support the American Friends Service Committee's work for world peace, particularly in response to the threat of nuclear weapons. The connection of this work with my personal history of escape from Nazi occupation is obvious, as is the effect of World War II on my extended family. I watch the world today and am horrified at how a rush to war is gaining support while more thoughtful political solutions are considered weak. Expanding nuclear arsenals cannot be ignored if humankind is to survive. This worry has consumed me to different degrees depending on what is currently happening on the world stage. Am I doing enough for peace and justice? Was this what I was destined for? I never clarified or consistently pursued an answer in those busy years on the job. Now the question I posed as a boy in England and a young man in college in Pennsylvania resurfaced in retirement as I recalled the past events and decisions of my life.

One of the joys of being retired is having time to travel. Carolyn and I made a major trip each year to several European countries as well as a long trek across the United States. I always thought I appreciated and respected similarities and differences of other cultures, but travel has a surprising way of opening one's eyes wider. I returned to the Czech Republic seven times over the years beginning in 1983 when the Communists were still in control. Each time I visited the Jewish quarter in Prague. At the Pinkas Synagogue I read through the names of Czech

Holocaust victims painted in small script, about one-half inch in size, on the inside walls of the building. It was sobering and terribly sad to realize that each listed name—and there were thousands—represented a life snuffed out. Walking into the synagogue with ceiling to floor names is overwhelming to the visitor. For me to suddenly recognize the names of my maternal grandfather and Jenda, the cousin I played with as a boy, quickly brought tears to my eyes. I identified the names of more relatives as I walked through the silence to other rooms. I thought back and imagined the scene of the last Kindertransport, the one with the most children. Children had said their good-byes to parents and relatives and were tensely settled on the train as I had been. But that train never departed Prague. A few months earlier my Kindertransport train brought me to safety and life. I was not forced off the train like those children that I saw in my mind because, in my case, the Nazis had not yet closed the Czech border. Those children were taken off and perished. Viewing the names on the old synagogue walls of innocent human beings who lost their lives reminded me that I escaped, begging the question again—"Why?"

Once when my cousin Paul was with us in Prague walking with me through the large park called Stromovka, we speculated about the possibility of living in the Czech Republic again. After articulating the reasons, pro and con, we concluded that America was now our home and our country. We agreed a major reason it would be difficult to spend a long amount of time in Prague again was the constant reminders of our family members who died. We expressed to each other how glad we were to be among those who escaped. Paul is a great friend and I remember how the bond between us strengthened on that walk. That first trip back to the old country was in 1983 with my mother. It was especially meaningful since she could answer so many of the questions that Paul and I asked. This first journey, while the Communists were still in power, gave us a basis of comparison for how the country was changing when we subsequently visited it six more times. Traveling in the Czech Republic had its lighter moments. On one trip when the country was still under Communist rule, I stopped by the side of the road to make certain the back door was fastened. As I was pulling out onto the four-lane highway a policeman pulled me over. "You did not look into your mirror when you pulled out and the car behind you had to swerve into the left lane," he informed me gruffly. After examining my international driving license and my passport, he continued, "I have to fine you ten crowns." That was less than one dollar and I dutifully paid then and there. He wrote out a receipt and as he handed it to me with my papers he said with a wry smile and a wink, "Next time we'll shoot you!"

I had another driving incident in Bratislava, Slovakia, where my aunt lived. I made a left-hand turn as I didn't see the sign prohibiting it. Suddenly, people on the sidewalk were sticking out their umbrellas into the street to slow me down. I eventually stopped after viewing in my mirror a hefty policeman running after me huffing noticeably. When he caught up to me he burst out with a torrent of abusive phrases in Slovak of which I understood not a word. Eventually he calmed down enough to say, "That will be ten crowns." Again I received a receipt for my on-the-spot payment and the matter was settled.

One of the early trips we made in retirement was to Florida to visit my cousin Paul. Carolyn felt relief in the warmth of winter months there from her atrial fibrillation and related heart problems. We purchased a double-wide stationary mobile home on the same street as Paul's and spent a few months each winter there in Florida. After Carolyn died, I sold the Key Largo residence and resumed living year-round in Hartford. That allowed me to strengthen my commitment to the Adult Learning Program, and over the next ten years I held several leadership posts. I sought to reorganize ALP for greater efficiency and to increase membership. Many members became new friends, and although I cannot claim social activism in my roles with this organization, I did work to schedule knowledgeable speakers to address inequities in the world and educate us about pressing present-day realities.

My last protest in the street was in 2012—demonstrating with Occupy Hartford over the growing rich-poor divide and the economic dangers of unrestricted big bank policies that aren't adequately curtailed to this day, thus posing ongoing risks in the country and stability worldwide. Now, my activism consists of writing letters to our national leaders and newspapers, signing a variety of petitions, and contributing money to causes I believe in. I try to remain optimistic that these actions do some good.

Retirement has been happy and fulfilling, although Carolyn's sudden death was a shock that led me to make numerous adjustments as a widower. One fortuitous event was meeting my now fiancée. Joy was returning to my life as I rang in the New Year of 2004 with Paula Karrh-McIntosh Fisher who was widowed two years before Carolyn died. Born and raised in New Mexico, Paula, like me, enjoys travel and is well-traveled. When we met, Paula had some familiarity with England, having toured the British Isles, later spending a summer in Bristol, England, doing a graduate course in medieval history. After growing up in Albuquerque, she lived in San Francisco, Hanover, New Hampshire, and White River Junction, Vermont, before receiving her baccalaureate degree with high distinction from the University of Michigan. Paula started her teaching career and a lifelong commitment to education in Ann Arbor, where her husband was completing a PhD. They settled in the Hartford area just a few years after Carolyn and I moved there with our three children. Following the deaths of our spouses, Paula and I both faced the challenges of newly minted singles after decades of being paired as married couples.

I learned later that men who lose their long-time partners tend to act sooner to fill the gap in their life than do women, and that proved true in our case. Before computer dating came on the scene, ads were placed in newspapers by those wanting to meet someone. Since the *Hartford Courant* ran such ads weekly, I decided to give this approach a try. Initially I answered a few ads under the heading *Women Seeking Men*; however, the preening and puffery of the writers quickly put me off. I decided to try placing an ad myself under *Men Seeking Women*. The first contacts were disappointing—conversation often bogged down and was centered on families I didn't know or repetitive stories about grandchildren. Once I had to endure a very long wait before the woman finally emerged, and it wasn't worth the wait. As it happened,

though, my ad appeared at the bottom of a column, right above an article Paula was reading one evening—and she took notice of it. She tells of
ripping it out and putting it in a drawer for almost three weeks. Finally
she called the number the paper listed and left a brief message to be for-
warded to me: her first name, the observation that the writer of the ad
and she seemed to have interests in common, and her contact number.
It was the shortest message I received from any woman! But our first
meeting almost ended before it happened. Paula was delayed getting
to our meeting place by a longer than usual wait at the dentist's office,
and this was a time before people carried personal phones with a log of
phone numbers in them, so I didn't hear from her that she was running
late. After waiting in the parking lot of my condo where we were to have
met, I had started to return to my condo when we encountered each
other at the lobby door—"Paula?"—"Ivan?" Once we connected, Paula
and I quickly found shared interests and points of view on a range of
subjects, and we discovered that our cultural tastes also synchronized.
We were interested in each other's history and enjoyed humor in similar
ways.

Together, we started attending concerts, plays, movies, dance pro-
ductions, and operas, and we visited museums. Our summers afforded
opportunities to garden, share outings with friends, and travel. In the
summer of 2004, we took our first long trip together to the beautiful
Gaspé Peninsula in Canada. One memory we recall was encountering
Canadians, even in some remote areas, who, seeing we were Americans,
approached us to express their dismay at the prospect of George W.
Bush being elected to another term as US president. Although we felt
a bond with them over this fear, we could only express back our same
concern! In recent years, Paula and I have taken one trip out of the
country each winter as a respite from indoor living. From April through
fall, my lifelong horticultural interest that started in England at Battle
House is sustained by working with Paula in her many gardens. I began
to enjoy cooking, initially following favorite recipes Carolyn had made
and some Czech recipes from my mother. I expanded my repertoire to
include many vegetarian menus, which Paula, being an animal lover,

heartily embraces. We instituted the tradition, still maintained, of a special Friday night dinner at my place. I assume the roles of chef and head waiter while Paula, who was often fatigued after a busy week before she retired, is happy to act as guest.

My story and the history surrounding it was reinforced earlier for Carolyn through trips to the Czech Republic and England, where we visited places and met people linked to my boyhood. With Paula, I have taken two trips to my homeland and worked on this memoir, and in so doing have opened my past to her too. It is our hope that this record will have value and be meaningful in some way to the readership of this book.

Reflecting on my activism, I realize that many of the decisions I made and actions I chose harken back to my essential question: My life was spared—was there a purpose? In one form or another, I tell myself, my undertakings can be interpreted as a response.

Chapter Fourteen: Am I a Jew? Am I a Christian?

⸻◆⸻

THE QUESTION OF identity as a Jew or a Christian in adulthood is sometimes asked, or at least wondered about, of escapees from the war in Europe who were Jewish children by birth but came in contact with different cultural influences, including religion, during or after their escape. The question "Are you a Jew or a Christian?" is seldom asked to me directly, but reading between the lines, some people who know my story obviously want to know. For me the response is that I am both and, in a sense, neither.

While this statement is accurate, it doesn't always feel like it fits. When I am with a group of people most of whom are Jewish and it is assumed that I am one of them, a voice inside says, "But I'm not." Similarly, when I am in a Christian setting such as occurs at a Christmas service, I sometimes feel that I am betraying my Jewish heritage. However, I never deny being a Jew or becoming a Christian.

Intellectually I find no fundamental incompatibility between Christianity and Judaism, since both believe in the Old Testament as sacred text, and all the disciples and Jesus himself were Jews. To my way of thinking, Jesus wanted to purify the Judaism of his day. The belief that Jesus was "the son of God" came later. But I have no desire for lengthy theological exposition. The persecutions that Jews suffered at the hands of Christians are a segment of history that did not have a prominent place in my thoughts about religion until recently.

My Jewish father recognized the universal beauty of the Christian Lord's Prayer; he told me that it is the most beautiful prayer ever written. When I talked with the nurse who was at his side when he died, she said it was that prayer he was reciting as he passed away.

My dual religious identity is seldom known to those around me, as I do not bring it up. Neither designation adds or detracts from who I am. My choices and actions reflect what I believe and reveal more about me than any label appended to me.

Chapter Fifteen: People, Places, and Things: An Update

———————◆———————

W HAT HAPPENED TO the people I mention in this memoir? How have places that played a role in my past and live on in my memory changed over the years? What cherished family possessions in Czechoslovakia made it to America? The updates in this section are organized sequentially by chapter.

Chapter One: The Kindertransport Kid, 1939

Children of Malva, Father's Sister
Eva, Malva's daughter and the oldest of my generation, was married in the mid-1930s to a businessman, Wilhelm (Wilda) Heller. They had a daughter, Janinka, youngest of the next generation and my Grandmother Bächer's first great-grandchild, who was fawned over by the whole family. The Hellers lived near us in Prague, and I sometimes stopped by to visit after school. Although Janinka was too young for me to play with, I loved to rattle toys to make her smile and admired the new life that had come into our family. In Terezín concentration camp, Janinka and the other children were encouraged to draw pictures, and later we saw hers in a published book of children's art from there. Janinka perished in Auschwitz with her parents.

Malva's other child was Wilhelm (Vilík), who was ten years older than me—I didn't know him very well. When I saw Vilík last he was in his army uniform and looked very formidable to me. He had wrapped his legs below the knees meticulously with the khaki bandage-like material that was the style of the day for some European armies. Vilík, too, perished, but his mother survived the horrors of Terezín and came to New York City to live with the Paul Backer family on 72ⁿᵈ Street. My father visited her practically every day.

Chapter Two: Childhood Memories from before the Nazis, 1929–1939

My Grandparents

Both my maternal grandparents from Dobruška entered Terezín in 1942, and Grandfather died there the following year. My mother visited Terezín with Carolyn, Paul, and me a year before she died. When we entered the crematorium and viewed the ovens where the dead were cremated and the ashes dumped into the river, she sobbed quietly, "So this is where my father ended up." Grandmother survived and returned home in May 1945, only to die from a burst appendix several weeks after her release.

My paternal grandmother died in her apartment in Prague in June 1940. During the war my family knew none of these details.

Aunt Vala, Mother's Younger Sister

Vala was an artist, known professionally as Valerie Jorud, and art attracted her to Berlin, one of the centers of European culture. Her two terracotta head sculptures of herself and my mother now sit proudly at either end of my bookcase as a constant reminder of her free spirit. Vala also sculpted in brass and made a chandelier for my family consisting of four twelve-inch figurines hanging upside down by their bent legs on a brass ring. The entire chandelier did not survive the war, but I rescued the four figures featured in it and mounted them on teak wood to make wall brackets. Two of them hang in my study face-to-face as acrobats swinging gracefully toward each other as if on a high circus wire or trapeze that they will ride forever.

But Vala's signature pieces were large cloth wall-hangings made with a solid background color onto which she sewed multicolored strips of materials, about an inch in width, in different patterns. I remember one unique work of reds, whites, and yellows with straight and angular configurations intertwined. Vala's artistic creations helped her eke out a meager living. Her income was supplemented by stipends sent by her parents and my mother. She worked in the studio of Jan Bontje van Beek, and Erich Heckel was her mentor.

I wondered—how did Vala, a Jew, survive in the Nazi capital? That question becomes even more puzzling since she was also a Communist sympathizer, perhaps a Party member. The explanation may be that her lover, a fellow sculptor named Hermann Bohlau, who was in the German army, shielded her. Bohlau was killed on the Russian front, but since he was away most of the time she had established a network of artists, and they seem to have helped her survive.

During the spring of 1945 Berlin was subject to deadly night air raids by allied forces, and on April 6, a month before the end of hostilities, Vala elected not to go to the air raid shelter in order to stay with an elderly lady who was not well enough to make the trip to the shelter. That night a direct hit on their building ended the life of my favorite aunt.

Aunt Mila, Mother's Youngest Sister

Mila survived in Bratislava and hid in the countryside of Slovakia where she was reunited with her husband, Boleslav. He was a partisan and was arrested and interred in Flossenbürg concentration camp. The account of his imprisonment and death march experiences in the spring of 1945 is recorded in his own words in Appendix 1. After Boleslav died in 1972, Aunt Mila came to New York several times to visit Mother and I, and my family always enjoyed her visits. Mila died of cancer in 1992.

Jirka, My Boyhood Friend

On March 15, 1939, everything changed. Jirka and I, ten-year-old friends, were standing side by side on the main street of our Prague neighborhood watching German troops march into the city. I was Jewish, he was not, and that difference determined the course our lives would take. Within two months I had been shepherded to England while Jirka remained in Czechoslovakia. I learned much later that my father had visited Jirka's father to ask if his son could leave with me, but the answer was no, and Jirka stayed home.

There was no contact between Jirka and me all through the war nor when the Communist party took over Czechoslovakia in 1948 and followed the Third Reich with another repressive regime. Not until the late 1990s did I track Jirka down. His English name, George Blaha, is not common in America. so when I heard that one of our astronauts went by that name, I immediately sent a letter addressed to him to the Houston Space Program. When I received no response, I concluded this was not my boyhood buddy.

A couple of years later, I saw the name again. This time it appeared in a New York Czech language newspaper article about a group of Czechs who erected a monument to freedom in Toronto. Jirka Blaha was listed. With renewed hope, I called the editor of the Toronto newspaper who directed me to a contact who knew the Blaha family. I learned they had moved from Canada to the now free Czech Republic, and I was given a phone number. My excited transatlantic telephone call was answered by a female voice who turned out to be Jirka's wife, and she said Jirka was training his hunting dogs, would be home in a while for lunch, and I should call again. Although cautiously optimistic that I had located my friend, I steeled myself that this might be another dead end.

When we finally spoke, I knew this was "my" Jirka. He was amazed how I tracked him down and was overjoyed to hear from me. He invited Carolyn and me to visit, and in 2000 we did. He met us at the airport holding a bright red rose and we drifted toward each other drawn by a mysterious force. I was touched when he presented the rose to my wife with a little bow. Sixty-one years had passed since we parted and yet we knew we were still friends. My heart beat a little faster as I gave thanks that my long search for Jirka ended in success.

Jirka and his spouse lived in Kostelec nad Labem, about fifteen miles from Prague. Their house had passed to them through an inheritance from Jirka's wife's side of the family and was originally a monastery. It had been renovated into a comfortable, spacious brick and white stucco dwelling, surrounded by several acres of land that included an orchard and a little farm with geese, ducks, rabbits, and a couple goats. We were enthralled with the history of the house, which included a secret underground passageway once used by monks, about half a mile long and now filled in, leading to a little Catholic church. One morning Jirka and I took a walk with his two hunting dogs he trained himself. One whistle, they stopped. Two whistles, they were off again. A long whistle, they returned immediately. I was very impressed.

During our weeklong visit I learned about Jirka's life during the intervening years since he and I last saw each other. We both survived perilous times. In his senior year in high school, Jirka wrote a satirical article about the Communists who had just taken control of the country. The authorities did not like it, and he was arrested and imprisoned. A whole decade was lost for Jirka until he was finally released, having been robbed of the joys and opportunities of early manhood, including marrying and having children. He took a job as a factory inspector. Living conditions became more relaxed and lenient in the 1960s leading up to the 1968 Prague Spring, but he was warned of the imminent Soviet Union invasion, so he fled to Canada. There he spent the next twenty-five years and learned English, but he longed for his homeland. He and his wife returned in the early 1990s with a Canadian pension, paid in dollars, that allows them to live in comfort, especially compared to many other Czechs.

Jirka's main interest in retirement is building a support group to help former prisoners of the Communists, as many of them are in a bad way. He stays active by keeping in touch with former inmates and providing assistance in any way he can. This has become his chief occupation and purpose in life. As we talked I realized that both of us value commitment to positive causes and act on what we determine to be important in life, each in his own way.

Our world views diverged significantly, but not surprisingly, due to our different experiences. Politically, he is more to the right and I more to the left, but we had little inclination to probe further. We shared our love of nature, ironic from two city boys, and I realized that our friendship transcended our differences. The visit reconnected and renewed a friendship after years of separate life journeys far from our homeland.

Chapter Three: The Rest of My Family Escapes, One by One, 1939

My Brother, Frank

After war broke out in September 1939, Frank volunteered for the armed forces and served in a Czechoslovak regiment attached to the British army. He was in France in 1940 when it fell to the Germans and later was awarded the highest French military decoration, *Croix de Guerre,* for bravery in escaping capture and overcoming obstacles to rejoin his unit. I familiarized Paula with the circumstances underlying this honor bestowed on Frank by the French government since he seldom spoke of it, although I know it meant much to him and he is appreciative. A few years ago on Czech Army Day, the Czech Embassy in Washington, DC, invited him and one other veteran to a reception in their honor to recognize their wartime service, and we attended the event. Frank took out his military decorations and wore them that day. I felt the same surge of pride in him as I had as a schoolboy in England when Frank was serving in the army. Toward the end of the war he participated in the encirclement of Dunkirk where fifteen thousand Germans eventually surrendered, then stayed in Europe to guide relief convoys of secondhand Buicks to Czechoslovakia. Being in Prague often enabled him to trace what happened to some of our relatives during the Holocaust and report back to the family now scattered across different continents. He made a special effort to visit the few members of our family who survived.

When Frank rejoined us in New York in 1947, he was horrified at my decision to become a Christian missionary. But all his entreaties to change my mind were in vain. For a year we shared a bedroom in our parents' apartment on Pinehurst Avenue in the Washington Heights section of Manhattan. We both studied there: he, at age twenty-six, at Columbia University, and I at Union Theological Seminary. But we continued to move in very separate worlds that rarely intersected.

Frank completed his degree in chemical engineering at Columbia University and later added a master's degree from Stevens Institute in Hoboken, New Jersey. The research facility at which he worked closed in 1971, and Frank, then age fifty, was unable to find employment in America. Making use of his foreign language skills, he moved to Zurich and later to Hamburg with the W.R. Grace Company. In the late 1970s he became the managing director of a company manufacturing adhesives in Tehran, Iran, mostly for the shoe industry. Mother visited him there and told fascinating stories about that country. However, with the Iranian Revolution of 1979 led by the Ayatollah Khomeini, Frank fled for his life once again, taking only suitcases and some Iranian carpets that he later was able to sell. The proceeds from the rug sales provided his living expenses. During the decade Frank lived abroad, I had little contact with my brother.

Eventually Frank returned to New York City to live and in 2002 he entered the Friends Retirement Community in Sandy Spring, Maryland, where he still resides. I am amazed how he has retained his lifelong zeal to be active and remains determined at age ninety-four to keep fulfilling goals he sets for himself. His present activities at the Quaker facility where he lives include being chair of the program committee, which arranges all variety of speakers for that community and also heading the nominating committee for the Czechoslovak Society of Arts and Sciences. But what really keeps Frank occupied is filing claims for the payment of insurance policies bought before the war by those who were murdered by the Nazis. He is driven by this commitment and feels each time a successful claim is paid to the victim's heirs that a measure of justice has been accomplished.

Paula and I follow a set routine, driving from Connecticut to Maryland twice a year for a visit with Frank over a long weekend. These are times to help Frank with errands and catch up with his friends and acquaintances and the one Czech relative in the area. During our stay, the three of us plan an evening out by carefully picking a quality movie to see then selecting a nice restaurant in the Washington area with a good wine list; it is a treat for us to us to see Frank enjoy a glass or two of wine on these occasions. Often we have a three-way discussion about the movie afterward. Frank is my closest relative, and I treasure these times with him.

The Chandelier and the Bookcase

As Mother recorded in her account about leaving Czechoslovakia, she had our furniture packed and crated to put in storage in a friend's garage. The most valuable pieces we owned were stolen during the war, but a few favorite household items survived and she had those shipped to New York. Among them were two family treasures, a chandelier and a bookcase, each having its own story.

The elegant chandelier graced our formal living room in Prague throughout those tranquil pre–World War II days. Light from its six gold-plated arms cast a subtle glow about the room. I used to gaze at it frequently, preferring to look toward the ceiling and examine its intricate design rather than practice my tedious lessons on the piano. But despite its striking presence, I never knew its history. Much later I learned that it originally hung in the dining room of my father's ancestral home in Kácov in the Czech Republic. In those days most light was from candles and the chandelier must have created a distinctive atmosphere suited for the Sabbath services held in that room. Somewhere in its history it was electrified and became a favored family possession. The chandelier survived the war and crossed the Atlantic with other saved furniture and was finally mounted to the ceiling in the living room of our New York apartment to illuminate it for the next thirty-six years until Mother died in 1984. When we closed her apartment, neither my brother nor I saw any way to incorporate the chandelier into our homes and since I owned a house we decided I should store it in my attic. It remained out of sight for eleven years until we were preparing to sell the house. Again, what to do with the fine old chandelier?

I very much wanted to sustain its useful life, so I decided to look for an organization that would respect the chandelier's history and value its Jewish origin from an earlier time. Luckily, the director of the Charter Oak Cultural Center in Hartford accepted it. Finally, our family's Czech chandelier had a new home lighting the stairwell in the renovated Center. The directors even approved an engraved plaque for the wall to inform all who read it of the chandelier's origin from the dining room/synagogue in Kácov. Every time I visit the Center for an event, I stop in the stairwell to fondly remember the chandelier's long journey and its place in my family's history.

• • •

A NEW BOOKCASE arrived at our apartment in prewar Czechoslovakia, and it was examined and approved by all. Custom-made of walnut, it was just the right fit for its spot in the library. Below the adjustable shelves for books was a cabinet with sliding doors, a perfect spot to hide things. Eventually the bookcase, like the chandelier, arrived in New York to be moved into a place of honor in Mother's bedroom. When I lived there, and later visited, I would sometimes stop to admire it.

When Mother died and my brother and I were dividing her belongings, I wanted the bookcase and so did he. But Frank wanted only a few things and I was taking most of Mother's possessions, so obviously it was only fair for him to get the bookcase. Later Frank moved into a retirement home, and Yvonne, the woman with whom he had lived for thirty years, refused to let him take the bookcase with him since he was leaving her and it was in her apartment. Years passed and Yvonne died. Frank could then reclaim the bookcase, but he couldn't fit it into his efficiency unit. So, it was finally my turn to take possession of the bookcase.

The trouble was that I knew I no longer needed another bookcase, and after doing some measuring, I realized I had no room for it. But still I wanted it. Why? The bookcase was showing its age, it wasn't in prime condition after so many moves, including the long transatlantic one, and

it certainly wasn't valuable. But I was obsessed with it and never enter-
tained the notion of leaving it. Then a solution presented itself. One of
my daughters was setting up a new household for herself, and I thought
she would surely take it. She agreed.

But how could I get this huge piece of furniture to another city from
the twenty-sixth floor of a New York City co-op apartment? For a single
piece of furniture I found moving companies to be prohibitively expensive, yet renting a U-Haul would necessitate finding strong helpers
willing to donate their time and labor to such an undertaking. Luckily
fortune shone upon me and my project when Yvonne's daughter moved
the bookcase with other furniture to her house outside of the city. My
good friend, Jim Reed, and his son agreed to help with the move using a
U-Haul van. On a cold November day following challenges I never want
to reenact, the bookcase passed to the third generation. It will stay useful and I will still be able to admire it from time to time.

Chapter Five: From School to School to School, 1939–1944

Hilton Hall
Carolyn and I drove up the winding driveway I had so often walked along
as a boy, and suddenly the big brick building popped into view. When
I first knew it, the building housed the school that the Czechoslovak
government in exile established for refugee children like myself. Now
it stood before me as a solid bastion of security. That is just how I felt
about Hilton Hall back in the days when I attended school in its stately
rooms. I recognized at once the remains of the stone balcony on the second floor, which collapsed under the weight of my friend who daringly
climbed out on it while the building was being converted into a school.

At the time, in our 1985 trip to England, my wife and I had stopped
at Hilton Hall as part of retracing where I lived after leaving my country
during the war years. Reaching Hilton Hall that calm sunny day, I parked
next to a flat-bed truck that was being swept out by a young man about
thirty. I wondered who was living there now and what Hilton Hall was
being used for. The young man jumped down from the truck, extended

his hand in greeting, and introduced himself as the son of Mr. Lewis, brother of the John Lewis I knew as a boy who ran the surrounding farm. Carolyn and I were delighted when the young Lewis invited us in to meet his parents, and I learned his father had served in the British army during the war. I felt a pleasing sense of continuity.

Inside of Hilton Hall I noted that the grand staircase seemed much smaller than I remembered, and I found the center hallway with its fireplace having just normal proportions although forty-three years earlier it seemed huge and outsized. No longer did it conjure up boyhood fantasies of knights gathered around a blazing fire with crackling logs twelve inches in diameter, or more. I was startled to discover that small metal plaques still remained fastened on each door with writing in Czech to indicate the use for that room: Dining Room, Music Rehearsal Room, Principal's Office, and Classroom. I was glad the Lewis family had not taken them down.

I learned that having the Czech school in their home fostered long-term relations between a few of the Czech teachers and the Lewises. Several members of the Lewis family had been to Prague and visited some of the staff members who had run our school. Mr. Lewis even spoke a few words of Czech and praised the beer in Czechoslovakia.

When I think back to my days at Hilton Hall, I can still see the cows being brought from pasture to be milked, the farm equipment strewn around, and John Lewis rushing around in knee-high rubber boots we called Wellingtons, trying to keep up with all his duties since he had no one to help him because most young men were fighting in the war. My visit to Hilton Hall filled me with nostalgia, and I reminded myself again how lucky I was to have been there.

Czechoslovak School in England Reunion in USA

It was entirely by accident that the reunion organizer found out from my brother that I had attended this school. I was interested in the event and decided to attend in October 2008. From the preliminary attendance sheet mailed beforehand, I recognized only two names but thought there would be others. As it happened, there were only two of us who had known each other. I had gone to the school when it opened its doors in the fall of 1940, and I left in 1942; the other eight students at the reunion went to the school after I had left, which explains why I didn't know them.

As the school grew it moved once more, this time to Abernant in Wales, and most attendees at the reunion went to that location. They were curious as to why I left the Czech school, and I was amused at their speculations that I might be the mysterious "bad boy" they heard about who was expelled. When I explained that my mother felt while we were in England I should have a "proper" English education, they shook their heads in disbelief. When they pressed me for more details about leaving the Czech school, I closed out the conversation with a somewhat curt, "because my mother made me go." I later wondered if one of the advantages of having gone to an English school at the insistence of my mother was that I did not have as pronounced a European accent when speaking English as did the others at the reunion.

I learned at the reunion that four of us had been "Winton kids" and escaped to England by the Kindertransports that Nicholas Winton organized. I also learned that while I was initially placed with an orthodox Jewish family, the Millers, the other three all went to Christian homes and talked about going to church and Sunday School with their families. They indicated that for the most part the new religion did not stick with them; although, like me, they were not raised as observant Jews. I am sure those wartime escapees were also cognizant as we talked that had it not been for Nicholas Winton and his trains, none of us or our descendants would be here today.

For many attending the reunion, it was their first trip to Washington, DC. Since there were no planned activities during the day, we made individual plans, going separate ways to sight-see. When I announced that I had two passes for the US Holocaust Museum if anyone wanted to use them, I got no takers; everyone felt such a visit would be too painful. Most had lost both parents in the war and I could understand their decision. The fact that my parents made it to England set me apart and was the subject of many survivor questions that were hard to answer knowing their circumstance.

The reunion did not provide the interaction among us that I hoped for. We came from different regions—Florida, Arizona, one person from Canada, another from England. We just didn't connect in the way of some school reunions. Thinking about this later, I concluded too many years had passed and we had little in common except for a few distant shared memories, tainted with sorrow, more than sixty years ago.

Chapter Seven: New York, 1944–1946

The Paul Backer family is often referenced in this chapter since we were closely intertwined in the early years after coming to America. Following is up-to-date information about individuals in this family.

Uncle Paul, My Father's Older Brother
My uncle remained head of the family until he had a massive stroke in 1948. It left him partially paralyzed and with a noticeable speech impediment, which he strove mightily to overcome with a therapist. I vividly remember his indomitable will to live and recover completely, but he never did and died in 1956.

Aunt Julia, Paul's Widow
Julia continued to live in the 72nd Street apartment until Malva, her sister-in-law and a Terezín survivor, succumbed to cancer in 1958. She then moved to a one-room house specially designed for her on a large piece of property owned by her son, also named Paul. Space was made available for her piano and harps. I was impressed by the comfort of the dwelling and how it fit her needs. Later she moved to a nursing home near Chicago, close to her daughter, Anna. In 1981 I was honored to officiate at her funeral, filled with specially selected music and poetry.

Charles, Paul's Oldest Son
After being discharged from the army, Charles studied at City College of New York and became a lawyer working in the insurance field. He died in 2008.

Paul, the Middle Child

My close friend was a mathematician, and a great lover of music. We lived near each other for six years in Key Largo, Florida, and he still resides in Florida. In retirement he earned a second bachelor's degree in botany, taught opera in his community, and loved to play bridge.

Anna, the Cousin Closest to Me in Age

Anna and her husband, Mark Perlberg, lived for a time in Japan and ultimately settled in Chicago, where she still resides. Since the death of Mark—an exceptional poet with several published books of poems to his credit—she and I have become close, speaking in Czech often to share thoughts about the present and our common past.

Chapter Ten: Being a Parish Priest and an Activist, 1963–1969

Harry Moniba and Family

After Harry lived with us in the Vicarage in East Rutherford in the 1960s, he returned to his native Liberia and taught school for a while. He then entered government service and spent several years in Washington, DC, as the first secretary in the Liberian Embassy, which also allowed him time to earn his PhD. I visited Harry and his growing family whenever I was in the nation's capital. His career progressed rapidly. Harry's custom was to call us on Christmas Eve, no matter where he was, and in 1980 he called to say, "I am now the ambassador to the Court of St. James in London. Wish me well."

Harry became vice president of Liberia in 1984, but when Charles Taylor overthrew the government Harry got his family out of Liberia, then fled the country himself. In 1992, his youngest daughter, named Koisay in Liberia, Americanized to Gladys, came to live with us in Hartford. Carolyn and I were empty-nesters and had plenty of room and were glad to welcome her. Koisay's arrival gave us a third daughter, and we assumed the role as active parents of a teenager again. She assimilated into our family quickly and over the years we met all of her four siblings. We started looking for the right school for Koisay and settled on the private Ethel Walker School in Simsbury for her final year in high school. The next fall "our daughter" entered Lafayette College in Easton, Pennsylvania. Koisay used her education in several career positions in the Greater Washington, DC, area and earned a master's degree in psychology.

Koisay's father, Harry, had run for president of Liberia in 1997 and was preparing to run again in the 2005 election. He was in the United States working toward that end when he was tragically killed in a head-on automobile accident on November 24, 2004. Harry Moniba was given one of the largest state funerals in the history of Monrovia, Liberia's capital. His family buried him in the family compound of their suburban Monrovia home. I am extremely proud to have been counted as one of Harry's close friends. He was a man of outstanding character who possessed a strong moral code and would have been, I am convinced, a dedicated and effective president for his troubled country, which faces great challenges in the twenty-first century.

In a sense upon Harry's death I became Koisay's surrogate father, and when she was married a few years later I had the privilege of walking her down the aisle along with her older brother to approving comments from the largely black congregation. I have visited Koisay, her husband, and her two children regularly in their suburban Maryland home and am proud to call her a member of our family.

AFTERWORD

———————◆———————

R EADING THE NEWS on my computer a few weeks ago in the same
squeaky old swivel chair where I learned about the attacks of
9/11, I found an uplifting column about a recent honor bestowed on
Nicholas Winton in my native Czechoslovakia. At observances of Czech
Independence Day in Prague on October 28, 2014, Sir Nicholas was
presented the Order of the White Lion, the highest honor of the Czech
Republic. Sir Nicholas was then 105. He was flown by the Czech Air
Force from his home in Maidenhead, England, to receive the honor
and be feted at Prague Castle with a few of his saved "children" looking on. As a fellow Czech octogenarian member of "Nicky's family" I
was touched deeply by this most recent recognition. Winton, always
reserved in discussing his inner and outer life, did give a few opinions
publicly in Prague, stated with typical brevity. Sir Nicholas himself did
not look back but rather pinned his expectations on future generations.
He hoped they would be inspired by his example—not to be onlookers
but to volunteer time and energy in the service of fellow human beings.
With many people across the world, I felt a great sense of loss when Sir
Nicholas Winton died in the summer of 2015 at the age of 106.

For me, writing this memoir has been an exercise in honest prob-
ing and introspection. The Kindertransport not only saved me from the
Holocaust but also determined who I became, as I have tried to live
responsibly on this planet. I began to address my natural disinclination to

tell my story, let alone broadcast it, and realized I still felt some boyhood shame for occasionally using my situation to elicit sympathy. For years I chose not to disclose my affiliations as both a Jew and a Christian, so this memoir resembles "coming out of the closet" in that regard, although any interpretation of deception or concealment on my part is not correct. As Nicholas Winton said, "I really didn't keep it a secret [his rescue activities]; I just didn't talk about it." The notion that people might genuinely be interested in learning about my past was brought home to me when I started to receive a few speaking invitations where I met new people. On a trip to Costa Rica with Paula, she mentioned something of my background in a dinner conversation, and those seated nearby were riveted by my brief summary and asked to hear more. Telling parts of my story in public has sharpened the focus of this memoir, and retirement has finally afforded me the time to write it.

Our uncertain future confronts burdens from the past. As the world lurches from one crisis to the next, I sometimes feel helpless and even, at times, hopeless. The example of Nicholas Winton's unrelenting determination to find solutions that help others motivates me to continue to be an activist.

TRAINS

Memories, distant yet fresh
Of trains from Prague
To visit grandparents and
Sled down long hills.

Train from Czechoslovakia
Longest and scariest, with other
Kindertransport young ones.
Through heart of Third Reich.

Arrive Liverpool Station,
Happy seeing my father,
But foster family,
Orthodox Jews, strange to me.

War erupts, another train,
London school children
Evacuated to Midlands for safety,
A new family home.

Attend two boarding schools,
One Czech, the other English,
Longer train rides ensue,
Bring sense of independence.

Wartime voyage across Atlantic,
Convoy zigzags
Two perilous weeks,
Thrills me, exciting adventure.

Land in Canada, overnight
Train to Montreal, enter United States,
Arrive Grand Central Station,
Discover world's largest city.

'Til now each train met by
Someone, known or unfamiliar.
Next train to College no one waits,
Now completely on my own.

Station in Pennsylvania recalls
Earlier station five years before.
Nervous and scared until
Seeing father and new family.

Years later, the *Shoa* film,
Holocaust victims sardined in
Cattle cars destined for gas chambers,
Recalled my escape.

Trains brought death to some,
For me life—saved from extinction.
The question haunts me still—
Why was I spared?

No explanation—
Blind chance or hidden design?
No answer satisfies.
I am forever grateful.

I strive for life of purpose,
Struggle for social justice
Answers my search for meaning,
Becomes my North Star.

———————◆———————

An Account of Imprisonment and a Death March, 1944–1945
by Boleslav Kubáček
Introduction and Translation by Ivan A. Backer

Introduction

Boleslav Kubáček was married to my mother's youngest sister, Mila. They were married in 1932 and had no children. He was a bank manager in Bratislava, now the capital of Slovakia. In 1939 Boleslav joined the resistance movement and his cell met at the bank where he was in charge. Their main activity was to help people escape from Czechoslovakia through Hungary and Yugoslavia to the West—England and America. A chain of people was involved. Those who needed help came to Boleslav's bank, and he took them to spend the night with others in the resistance. Some stayed with Boleslav and Mila. Those fleeing would be escorted across the border to Hungary.

Everything was kept secret until 1944 when a traitor infiltrated the cell leading to the arrest of Boleslav and his collaborators on October 13 by the Nazis. He was put in solitary confinement, and his friend Bochan was imprisoned separately. They were allowed no visitors.

Both Boleslav and Bochan were transferred to a prison in Brno, the capital of Moravia, where daily executions were taking place. In Brno,

Boleslav was to be confronted by the man who betrayed the group. Boleslav was most afraid of him since he knew the betrayer had proof of the activities. The confrontation did not happen; instead Boleslav was sent to a concentration camp.

Imprisonment
Boleslav's account begins with two quotations:

> *"Fret not yourself because of the wicked,*
> *Be not envious of wrongdoers!*
> *For they will soon fade like grass*
> *And wither like the green herb."* (Psalm 37:1)

> *"I firmly believe that after the current suffering,*
> *The government over your affairs*
> *Will return into your hands*
> *O Czech people!"* —John Amos Comenius

I begin this account [as a letter to his brother] with the quotation from Psalm 37 by which I tried to live long before I was arrested, and which sustained me during my years of imprisonment. The same is true of the faith Comenius had in the renewal of our freedom.

A day in prison is interminably long. For two months I was in solitary confinement, as was Bochan. What thoughts haunted our minds— worry about our own future and that of those dearest to us. Everything that I had with me in Brno reminded me of my home and the painstaking hands of my wife, who hoped for my return. But I was in the clutches of the Gestapo monsters. In the corridor I heard the screech of the metal reinforced boots of the guards, and their blows and swearing at prisoners. I was reminded of the heading to Dante's description of hell, "All hope is lost."

On December 11, I am led to a larger cell for six people. Bochan also is put in a similar cell, but a different one. This happens after both Bochan and I are cross-examined by the Gestapo. On Christmas day we receive a piece of dry bread and a cup of pea soup with barley that is full of little beetles.

I am called in the evening of January 23, 1945, with the words "everybody out." What now? Am I going home, to a concentration camp, or to be executed? Bochan is called from the other cell, and in the corridor he says with his usual smile, "So doctor [Boleslav was a lawyer and therefore a doctor of jurisprudence], we are either going to a concentration camp or to the wall [to be shot], but in any event let it be over." He is suffering from the shock of the most immediate executions. A young partisan from his cell is a very recent victim. Fifteen minutes after he is called, he is in his shirt at the execution site and one of the monsters shouts, "We want to see blood." The execution site is under a mosaic of Saint Wenceslas with the heading, "Don't let us or our future perish." These cruel destroyers!

During the night from the 23rd to the 24th of January, Bochan and I are finally together for a few hours. We whisper about our experiences but are wary of making any noise. Bochan reminisces about his wife and son and says that he is glad that they have left Bratislava because he was uneasy there when he saw his wife having to cope with his absence. We hope for a happy ending. Heeding my advice, Bochan puts on warm underwear to brave the frost of the next morning. In the early hours they push us into a bus to take us to the railroad station.

As we leave the bus I get my first blow with a rifle butt—so that I will move faster. We are put into a rickety old freight railcar, but it does have a roof. The SS guarding us are swinging their rifles whether they hit heads or something else. Forced to sit on the floor, pressed together like sardines, I sit on someone's legs, and mine are similarly occupied. After a while I don't feel the pain any longer. It is cold, and at six o'clock we start to move west. The train stops briefly in Prague at the Wilson station, but then it is on toward Pilzen and Cheb. We huddle for warmth during the night and lend our one pair of gloves to another prisoner to warm his hands.

A German troop transport goes by. Germany is still not finished. But we speculate that the end of the war will come between the middle of April and May. We set the terminal date at May 13, since we count the months from our arrests on October 13. After three days on the train without a drop of water, and no food or sleep, we alight. There are about eight hundred of us, and the SS are swearing and swinging their rifles. It is snowing, and the ruins of a castle are visible on the horizon as we are ordered to march. The road is uphill, and I am carrying my suitcase, but I feel weak from the journey and am getting short of breath. A strong fellow prisoner helps to carry my suitcase. God reward him if he still lives, and if he does not, may he rest in peace and be forever praised. At last we reach our goal, the concentration camp.

Flossenbürg

Our whole transport stands in front of the building that houses the disinfectant facilities and warm showers. Marched inside where it is warm from the steam of showers, the Nazis take a roll call to make sure that no one is missing. Already we see the everyday sight of shadows that pass for people, dressed in striped prisoner garb, as with unsteady steps they carry stretchers from the barracks. On them lie the remains of what used to be human bodies, covered with yellow skin marked by black blotches from the wounds of the guards. Their heads are covered with a dirty blanket. Thus ends the earthly pilgrimage for about 150 people every day.

Following the roll call we are marched into another building, where we have to strip. I can't believe my eyes. Those who came before us are completely naked and barefoot and are forced to run outside across the snow. Shaken by this sight and surprised by the horror, we wonder what this means. But there is no time for explanations because it is my turn. The vile guards are shouting at everyone and a few feet ahead I see an older, blond SS officer waving and striking with his whip to make us undress quicker. We can keep only those personal items that will fit into the palm of one hand. All our clothing, underwear, and shoes go in one pile. Money, jewelry, and anything else of value are to be surrendered separately. There is no time to think as the belts and whips descend. I throw away my hat, my suitcase, and undress as fast as possible. I remove my watch from my trousers, but what should I save? Quickly I take a photo of Mila and me and put it into the glasses case. I also take two pieces of soap since that is most important in prison, next to bread. I am standing on a cement floor, naked and barefoot, in an unheated room with the window wide open. Shivering, my mind wanders to Mila and all my dear ones, amid the uncertainty of what these devils have in store for us. My anger grows at this cruelty and humiliation. If my mother saw me now her old heart could not stand it.

Then I am forced to run to the baths like Adam through the snow and frost. I am holding all my worldly goods—my glasses, toothbrush, and two pieces of soap—one of which a Polish guard steals. We are pressed in like a herd of cattle, prodded along by young Polish and Russian boys who are also prisoners but do the bidding of the Germans with whips of rope and belts having braided split ends. They also steal our food and extract other things. They are as cruel and hateful as the Germans. Perhaps the explanation lies in their long incarceration in the concentration camp. Among the Russians there is now and then a decent person, but not among the Poles.

Now they cut our hair, more like plucking them from our bodies because their scissors are so dull. Bales of hair are then carried out. We are in line to receive clothing, nothing more than rough rags that itch, and these we put on our wet bodies. I receive ladies panties instead of men's, a short-sleeved undershirt that reaches to the middle of my stomach, old patched overalls that reach to the middle of my calves, and a summer coat that might fit a fifteen-year-old boy. That is our entire wardrobe—nothing for the neck or head—no handkerchief or towel.

After the warm shower we stand outside again in a freezing wind. I feel a blow on the back of my head as a seventeen-year-old Pole asserts his authority. At last, in the late afternoon, they take us to Building 20, and we are shown our places. The building is filled with tri-level beds with narrow passageways between them. Bochan and I share a bunk, along with an engineer, Uher, from Brno. The bunks are about 72 centimeters (29 inches) wide, shared by three people. In some there are four and sometimes even five people. Those not on the top bunk endure the dirt dropping from the straw above, and sometimes the bunks collapse and people are hurt. It happened to me twice.

Shortly after that we are again chased outside for another roll call. We have been here since the morning and still have had nothing to eat or drink. There are eight hundred of us lined up, hardly able to stand on our feet. We look like scarecrows in the rags we are wearing. It is freezing, and the wind is sharp as the first stars appear. Still we wait, shivering with cold, hungry, standing on one foot then the other so as not to freeze. We are suffering from the cold, from hunger, from sleep deprivation, from the haircut and warm shower, dressed in rags. There is still no sight of the commanding officer to end the roll call. I concentrate all my strength not to fall; looking at the stars I plead: "God, punish these Germans. Even if I have to die in this great conflict that I find myself in, hear my plea, O God!" When the roll call ends we get some lukewarm tea, but nothing to eat. So ends our first day in Flossenbürg.

After three days we finally get something to eat. Then we are instructed that in the evening no one can leave the barrack. For a minor infraction we can get twenty-five or fifty lashes of the whip, and for more serious offences, death. If someone has to use the latrine during the night, they must first report to the guard on duty so that he can alert the guards outside, since they have orders to shoot anyone on sight that does not have permission. And if someone has an accident before reaching the latrine he will get fifty lashes. I fall asleep amidst worries about the future here and concern for my loved ones.

The first days in the concentration camp have a similar routine: roll call, medical classification, a very quick shower, constantly speeded up by the guards, and then a medical exam by one doctor for eight hundred prisoners. He looks superficially to see that we have a head and every limb and wrote a classification in red. Bochan receives a one (the highest ranking) and I [receive] a two. At least four times a day we are driven outside to stand in the cold. At night in small groups we gossip about the day's events. Once in a while someone smuggles in a newspaper.

In the morning the whip augments the alarm clock to move us faster. We are getting used to the dirt and cold. Whenever possible we get into bed to keep warmer. Our barrack is under the charge of a man who killed his parents and was sentenced to life imprisonment. On the whole he is fair, but he can wield the whip. The first whipping I witnessed was of two boys, for whose misdeeds eight hundred of us had to stand in the freezing cold for a half hour before roll call. After the third blow, one fell and screamed like an animal. After a while a person gets used to such sights. During the next two months every morning I see blood flow and people beaten to death. One walks among the dead without interest, because one sees, so to speak, one's own grave. A box of matches has more value than a human life.

The second day after our arrival one of the more curious prisoners makes a discovery. With a terrified look he tells us that behind the fence near the latrine there is a heap of bodies. I was never curious about such unforgettable sights, and I was not in a spiritual condition to yearn to see it, but in the end I have to convince myself that the sight is real, and I look through a hole in the fence. At the edge of the forest, about three feet in front of me, there is a heap of bodies, partially covered by snow. The majority are naked; here and there an arm or leg protrudes. The suffering and terror of dying is all too evident on their faces. I quickly turn away; it is difficult to look at the glassy stares.

This is happening to people in the twentieth century, in Europe, the cradle of Christian civilization. They end up as a heap of logs. I meander back to the barrack. These are people who not long ago lived normal lives, like I did; who loved and were loved; who earned their daily bread and enjoyed life's joys. "O God, grant that I may not end up this way, but your will be done!" If this lasts much longer more of us will find ourselves on this heap. Already many are going to the latrine frequently and returning with a sick expression.

At the roll call the next day a thick smoke coming from the vicinity of the latrine chokes us. The stench is from the rags and bones of the heap of corpses being burned. It becomes an everyday occurrence about which we complain that it should not stink so much. People are becoming accustomed to the horror that ends lives.

The latrine is visited more often, and we don't dare to admit how many times we have been there. Bochan has a fever and angina pains. When he begins to recover the same thing hits me. Whenever possible I am lying down and giving my food to a young man in the next bed whom I helped in 1940 to cross over into Hungary.

The first transport for a work assignment is being organized, but it is impossible to find out details. Bochan is called and thus ends our being together. This happens one Sunday in the middle of February, when those chosen are lined up for a shower and issued the striped prison uniform. We say good-bye in case we do not meet again. I still have a fever and angina pains. Bochan has now recovered and is quiet but on the whole optimistic. "After all it can't be worse than in the camp." How naive! Those criminals are not concerned about maintaining people in a condition to be able to work. They only want to get the maximum out of you until you collapse. But we both believe that the war can't last much longer. The Russian offensive is proceeding well, and we hope for our return and to be free of this place surrounded by barbed wire. The thought that we are being separated for a long time does not enter our heads. The end has to come within two months and surely we can bear it for that long.

The Monday morning after our good-bye our barrack has its first death. He was an older man who could not withstand the dysentery. No one takes much notice. But the stench in the barrack increases and now even the younger ones are catching it. It is freezing at the latrines, and the outside spigots for washing have ice underneath them. When one has to go to the latrine and sit several times a night, one worsens, especially since being sick already began by catching a cold on the journey from Brno.

In the afternoon they begin to divide us according to the alphabet to take us to other barracks. Barrack 20 has to be emptied to make room for a new transport. But under the 'Ks' my name is omitted. What does it mean? When I report it I am told that they did not forget about me, and I am included in the last section. We leave our barrack in the late afternoon and are joined by prisoners from another building. First come the sick ones and they make a moving picture: most are bent to the ground with pain, supporting each other as they drag themselves forward slowly. A seriously sick prisoner is in our group. He is so weak from the dysentery that he cannot control himself. He is terribly dirty since he can no longer drag himself to the latrine. First they drag him, but then they conclude that it makes no sense as he is going to die any minute anyway, and they put him back into his stinking bunk.

We ascend a steep hill to Barrack 9. I don't know a soul, and that is a great loss. Living in 9 is the worst time for me at Flossenbürg. In 20, we had assigned bunks, but here you don't know where you are going to put your head or whether you are going to be able to sleep. And sleep in the concentration camp is as important as food. The whip was used only to move us along in 20, but here it rains down all the time, and one never knows from which direction to expect the next blow.

The conditions in Barrack 9 are terrible. I had a serious case of bronchitis and a cold from the freezing conditions to which we were exposed. The food is awful and sleep almost nonexistent. If one cannot find a place on a bunk, one has to sit all night in the little alleys between bunks, pressed together like sardines. And the whip is used constantly, along with punches and kicks. Shortly afterward, I have an opportunity to speak to Bochan, through barbed wire. He is in Barrack 17, dressed in his prisoner uniform, and awaiting a transport. He seems to be in good condition, both physically and spiritually, but in comparison I am a beggar. I am exhausted from lack of sleep. We discuss our situation and he is glad to be leaving the camp hoping that conditions outside will improve, and with his usual smile he adds, "I can stand as much as the others, and this can't last much longer."

He left shortly after that. We were such good friends and I mourn his end very much. We were looking forward so much to returning to our native land, and I still don't want to believe that he is not coming back. But the prisoners' work was making people fall like flies, and it overcame even strong, healthy men. He caught pneumonia and that was the end.

After Bochan's departure my turn comes. About twenty-five hundred men form new work forces. I am in the first contingent of about five hundred men. On February 20, we march out of the yellow gates of Flossenbürg in our striped prisoner rags. For good luck I make sure that I step out on my right foot. In my pocket I have saved a piece of bread, and I have my glasses, soap, and toothbrush—all my worldly possessions. They even make us surrender our old rags when they issue the prison uniforms. In place of the undershirt I had, they give me a piece of rough cloth with a hole cut out for the head and arms. I have one pair of socks.

It is about five o'clock in the afternoon, the February sun is shining, and it is not so cold in our "new" clothing. We leave the camp and the barbed wire fence that I hope to God that I will never see again. We march through the little Flossenbürg village to the station. At the church I see a crucifix, and I pray: "Lord Jesus Christ, who art the Son of God, have mercy on me."

Open fields surround the station, appearing gray with almost no snow left on them. But I catch a glimpse of the first snowdrop—the first sign of spring. I am glad to be outside of the fence and away from Barrack 9, where there is an outbreak of typhus. After waiting a while we climb into the cattle cars, and in the process someone steals my bread. I hope that I will withstand the hunger. But the main thing is that I can no longer see the guard towers with their mounted machine guns.

We get the order to sit on the floor just as we were instructed on the trip from Brno. But now I am among strangers who do not give way, so people fight for a little space. We are now only half human—eat or be eaten. We seek permission to stand for a while to help our circulation. It is denied and we spend a miserable night with aching legs. Snow falls during the night. The next morning we are at the station in Plattling. At noon we are given bread and cheese, but nothing to drink. Everything disappears quickly since we have not eaten for twenty-four hours. We are glad when we finally leave the train late in the afternoon and march into town. On the square the German women laugh at us. I think, *You girls are spiritually prostituted by Hitler, but your time is coming soon. Your comeuppance will make you cowards and you will be brought low.*

We are marching through melting snow and mud. Going through a neat little Bavarian town, passing the church, we turn toward a school. In front of it there is a roll call, after which they send us inside in small groups. The classrooms have beds, again in tri-levels, but there is fresh straw and blankets. And only two of us will share each bunk. At last I will have a good sleep. I am to share my bunk with Mr. Weiner from Bratislava. But a little later others are assigned to our room and I gain another bedmate, a dental technician from Krakow. He offers me some raw beets that I accept gingerly and chew very thoroughly, hoping not to get diarrhea from them. It is the first vegetable in four months, and I accept them gratefully. We are again given bread with margarine, and after my previous experiences I have learned to eat it at once before it is stolen. As the saying goes in the camps, "Don't save for tomorrow what you can eat today, before it is stolen."

The majority in our work unit are Jews: more than two hundred from Poland, eighty-four from Czechoslovakia, and the rest from all over Europe. For supper we get hot vegetable soup. We also receive our own metal cup, and that is a major improvement since in Flossenbürg there were few utensils, and when the first people were finished they had to give up their plate, which probably was an old rusty metal thing, and the next person would then eat from it. It goes without saying that it was not washed. I fall asleep with a good feeling.

When the camp's supervisor learns that I was an attorney he indicates that he will make me a "reporting clerk," a position that in concentration camps can be of some importance, depending on circumstances. Keeping his promise, my fellow Czech prisoners have very long faces when they see me the next day working at his table. They generally consider me a stupid man, since I have not succumbed to the camp's immorality and have remained a decent person. By this assignment I am saved from heavy labor and daily beatings. I get my own bed, outside the common area. I receive a little more food, and although I am still hungry at times, most of the time it is enough. I begin to regain some of my weight, and my cold finally goes away by the beginning of April. I would not have believed how much pus a runny nose could produce in a person!

The conditions in Plattling are very difficult. Although the food is a little tastier than in Flossenbürg, there still is not enough of it, especially for the heavy labor. We are awakened at 4:00 a.m. summer saving time, and at 5:00 during the winter. At each morning roll call for work assignments, blood flows, and people die daily. One kapo, imprisoned for murder, kills two people in a single afternoon, and boasts that he has killed 140 people altogether. I am unable to prevent any brutality, since the SS commander of our unit endorses these incidents. In the camp the rule of might and terror prevails. I am able to disarm the kapos by being respectful and quiet, and they do not bother me. They are also aware that through my duties I am in daily contact with the SS chief and his deputy, and the kapos themselves might be in jeopardy for any physical harm to me. That condition of course does not exist for other prisoners.

In Plattling I see the dead and the sick at each inspection, at least ten times a day, and witness how people in concentration camps suffer from hunger and infected deep wounds. And still they have to go to work with holes in their bodies. One person has several feet of gauze stuffed in such a wound. What pain he must have endured when the doctor removed it and then pressed a new similar dressing in. At each roll call people lay down with pussy fingers and legs, infected to the bone. That is of little concern to the Nazis, and they receive no care. In my former life I could not stand to look at a less serious wound, but now I even learn to eat watching such sights. A person becomes used to it under these condition. Typhus breaks out in the camp, but fortunately there are only three cases. I could write much more about Plattling, but we are ending our stay here and on April 24, 1945 we have to leave.

Death March

Already by the middle of April many of the older prisoners, mostly Jews, feared that they might again experience another death march. They had already survived a three-week march from Auschwitz, sometimes on foot and at times in open wagons with a heap of dead bodies. Tired as they were they had sat on the bodies and even slept on them. It was rumored that the SS might shoot us before fleeing themselves as the American army advanced. The Jews were particularly upset. I tried to assure them that the Germans must realize that they have lost the war and that they will not want to add to their already huge war crimes.

But when a prisoner, Tonda Bondy, returns from his work assignment on Sunday, April 22, and tells us that he has seen fifteen prisoners shot by the side of the road, less than two kilometers away, even I start to have doubts. It is a miserable prospect to have survived the entire war only to be shot in the end.

At the roll call on April 24, after three more prisoners have just died, Tonda tells us: "I just saw four SS officers visit our commander. They were escorting about five thousand prisoners when the Americans surrounded them and arrested everyone. Only they had managed to escape. The Americans are only about 40 kilometers from us and they had even penetrated to Straubing before they withdrew. I think, my boys, that we are going to march out of here and I am dreading it as I recall the march from Auschwitz, and the corpses I saw on Sunday."

I hurry to the office to tell my friend the other clerk, a Czech Jew named Honza Schneider. He has already survived both Terezín and Auschwitz. Then I see our superior go to the camp commander, and he soon returns with an order to burn the catalog of all prisoners, pack other incriminating evidence, and prepare for the march. I am already packed. So are all the kapos, who packed a week ago and now go around the camp in civilian clothes without their prisoner numbers. The prisoners from work sites are recalled, and everything is being readied for our departure. I have three blankets and one set of dirty underwear. There is a great demand for civilian clothing.

After Plattling was bombed, our superior brought an almost full sack of semolina or polenta to the office. As the prisoners prepare for departure, Honza Schneider and I cook the pudding, and we fill ourselves even though it is as thick as cement. We even take some with us on our plates as provision for the journey. I also have a piece of bread in my pocket.

Dr. Jedlička is a Polish medical doctor and has been a prisoner since 1939, and he is a very decent man. He, Honza, and I debate whether it would be better to hide ourselves in the camp and wait a few days for the Americans. Jedlička shows us that under his prisoner garb he has civilian clothing. He offers to register me as being sick, but he doesn't try to convince me since another possibility is that the SS will shoot everyone left in the camp. I give him the addresses of Mila and my mother in case he gains freedom faster than me. I ask him to write to them, in case I do not return and instead end up shot in some ditch, that they might know that during those last few weeks I was in fairly good shape. The doctor is ordered to remain in the camp to care for the sick. He was my true friend and perhaps God spared him. We part with deep feeling for each other.

In the camp everything is topsy-turvy. The younger prisoners welcome the march as an end to their heavy labor, but the older ones are worried since they recall the 120 kilometer journey from Auschwitz in the frost and snow, the open rail cars with their mounds of dead, and being without food. Our superior got drunk, and the other SS officers finished all the alcohol around. We are ordered to march smartly through town, but he himself cannot talk or march straight. He swears at us all the time, but we largely ignore him.

We are grouped together, counted, and ordered to march. I am in the first five-man line with Honza and Dr. Rottenberg, a Belgian Jew. We look back fleetingly at the camp as our sick friends stand in front of their barracks, and wonder if we will ever see each other again.

Left, left, left! The marching orders are barked out by kapo Hans. On the whole he is a decent man who does not strike us without reason. He reminds us in front to go as slowly as possible so that the sick in the rear can keep up. He says that we should ignore the mad rantings of our drunk superior who wants us to "parade march." We in front are in a predicament. Our superior is constantly urging us to look smart marching through town, and we are conscious of those in the back. So we take steps, as short as we can. In town we feel how close we are to the front, since there are soldiers, ambulances with their Red Cross, and army equipment everywhere. By the railroad station there is also evidence of the recent air raid in which one thousand people, including soldiers, died. Many civilians and soldiers crowd around the shops.

At an intersection in town we bear left, and on the yellow sign it says: "Landau, 23 km." [See map.] It is late afternoon and we are coming to open fields. The sun has come out, and in my heart I feel lighter, as when a person first encounters nature on a spring day after a long confinement. Honza and I are still full from the cement-like semolina. My three blankets are thrown over my shoulder, my cup is attached through a button hole, and on my plate there is still some semolina. My worn-out boots leak water through the bottom, but a shoemaker repaired the tops the day before we left, so that at least keeps out the sand and stones.

The larks are singing and I am under the impression that I am on some kind of outing. Soon I hear gunfire on the sides and in the back but the SS are with us in front. I have the impression that someone is hunting rabbits, just as the guards did on the last day before we left Plattling. We conclude that discipline is disappearing since Germany has strict laws against hunting, although Field Marshall Goering is the imperial hunter.

On the horizon appear three planes, as in the distance a small farm and a hamlet with a church becomes visible. We are ordered to disperse in the fields and lie down. I take refuge by turning right and lying down in some clover on a ridge next to the railroad tracks. The planes veer in the opposite direction. Suddenly there is a loud explosion and the farm and hamlet vanish in a thick cloud of smoke and fire.

Near me is a small viaduct, and it would be possible to hide there and cross into the fields on the other side. The thought of freedom is very inviting. But I don't know if at the next assembly we will be counted again, in which case my absence would soon be discovered, since I am in the first row of marchers and the commandant and most of the guards know me. And then where could I flee in my prisoner's uniform and with a bald band on my head, where they cut my hair. If they caught me, and that is highly likely, I would be shot on the spot. We were warned against this before we left camp.

After the air raid we are ordered to reassemble and resume the march. In another half an hour we are again ordered to lie down in the fields as the air raids continue throughout the afternoon. More gunfire by the guards is heard as we continue. As we approach the village Wallersdorf, about 12 kilometers from Plattling toward Landau, we learn that the guards have been shooting the sick prisoners. Already, during the first two hours of the march, twelve prisoners have been killed, among them several Czechs. Anyone who cannot go further is shot. So it is not rabbits that are being hunted, but peoples' wretched earthly journey is ended a few days before the end of the war—some of whom have been in the concentration camp four and a half years and were awaiting being freed.

In Wallersdorf we rest, to give our commanders time to decide whether the march should go on or we should spend the night here. There are many troops in the village. In the end we turn toward the station, go under the tracks, and stand again on the other side. There is a fairly large grassy depression in which it would be easy to herd us to sleep. It would be an easy place to guard, but because the guards would also have to sleep outside and a cold wind is blowing from the north we return to the fields where there is a large barn.

There we each receive a little bread before beginning a mad scramble for a place to sleep. We all want to be comfortable, and there are many arguments. Everyone knows that sleep is very important, and who knows when we will be eating or sleeping next. Honza, Tonda, another prisoner from Nachod, Egon Horpaczky, and I form a little group because it is a little easier to survive. A person alone is lost, as I well remember from Barrack 9 in Flossenbürg. As we prepare our lair for the night, we share our blankets—Honza and I have three each and the others only one— and we have a little fight with three nearby Frenchmen who try to elicit our sympathy by recalling the historic friendship between France and Czechoslovakia. Eventually we settle the conflict. I tell them that it is uncomfortable for us to be arguing with them since we are all oppressed under the boot of Germany.

I put my towel, my little bundle of clothing, and what remains of my semolina under my head as we fall asleep, dressed without boots on. In an alcove of the barn there are still four corpses from previous transports that had spent the night here before us. So we sleep together, the dead and the alive, without any sentimentality. After all many of those who started out with us in the morning now lie shot along the roadside we traveled. And any of us may meet the same fate in the coming days. In spite of sore feet caused by miserable boots we keep trucking further.

We are roused quickly in the morning with shouts, "Everybody up!" My plate with the semolina is missing; only a bit of the paper in which it was wrapped is found in the straw where our French neighbors were sleeping. It was consumed during the night as proof of the historic Franco-Czech friendship. The Frenchmen quickly disappeared in the morning, but I find them in the afternoon and tell them they are thieves. This, however, does not satisfy my hunger.

There is nothing for breakfast, but I still have the bread in my pocket from yesterday. Now in the morning I feel rested and that is almost like being full. But I will be hungry after marching for a few hours, and then the bread will come in very handy. We pass through a village full of soldiers, past an airstrip, and cross the river Isar into the small town of Landau. There I see a truck with a group of our ill prisoners from Plattling. Why are they dragging these poor souls with us? Before we cross the bridge I eat my bread. Around the road there are tank traps, and the fields have been mined. Beyond Landau we see burned out cars and dead horses. Beside one car I see a burned skeleton, next to which stands a rifle with a helmet on it. It is there probably in respect to the burned soldier.

We meet a group of Hungarian soldiers, and each one has one or two loaves of bread. It is already afternoon and we have been marching since morning, without anything to eat since the piece of bread we got last night. We are hungry as tigers. The shots we hear from the rear spur us on. If one does not endure one gets a bullet in the head along the road. Here death has already visited us from airplanes that targeted a group of soldiers. So no one will be surprised to see a few more corpses.

At about two o'clock in the afternoon we head toward a woods with a brook running next to a meadow. Rest! The sun is shining, and we stretch out on a little rise. Honza brings out the semolina he has left, and our little group consumes it all. Then, one by one, we go to the stream to wash ourselves after a very long time. There was no water in the concentration camp for the last week, because, we were told, the water supply was damaged in several places during an air raid. Washing ourselves was accompanied by hunting for lice. All of us are infested with them, and the lice are even multiplying on our bodies.

We get some "soup" at 4:00 p.m. and then march on. We pass artillery units camouflaged by the side of the road. One of our Hungarian Jews learns from a Hungarian officer that the front is only about 50 kilometers away. In the village of Simbach there is a short break, and we receive a can of food to share between two of us. We eat it cold without bread. I hope it does not make us sick. We spend the night there in a barn. Tonda Bondy tapes up my sore leg with a bandage he saved. He remembers from previous marches how important bandages are on marches. That is the last day we eat something. During the night three kapos and two SS officers disappear. It is easy for them to escape since they are German and have civilian clothes, as well money, watches, and jewelry all stolen from prisoners. It is a sign of the declining morale and general deterioration.

In the morning we crawl out of the straw. There is nothing for breakfast so we set out on an empty stomach. In a little while we are again lying in the grass as airplanes circle above us. We turn sharply to the west, cross through a wood, and breathe the invigorating morning air. As we skirt another small town we meet other prisoners everywhere, all in the same fix as we. One group of young Jews is even singing as they march in the opposite direction from us. Some poor soul throws a box of biscuits out of a window. The prisoner who catches it is clubbed to death with SS rifle butts. Such is our "escort."

As we march on, we skirt the town of Schöenau. The roads are jammed with troops, and with discarded weapons—another good sign. As it begins to rain we find another barn to rest in. Our little group finds a patch of dry clover to climb in. Tonda Bondy is tempted to remain in the barn and disappear. We are all slowly agreeing to flee, but only when there is a good opportunity. It will be difficult for four of us to escape together, but I would not like to do it alone since it is such a huge risk.

As we leave we are each given some soup with polenta and one potato. Then we march on, but slower and slower. We are in a hilly country, going down and then up again. It is difficult to march being hungry, and the blankets are becoming heavier. Tonda Bondy finds a beet along the road, the size of a matchbox. He cleans it off, divides it into four parts so that we can each have a mouthful. But it isn't enough for starving men who have had no bread for two days.

It is already nine o'clock as we pass through the town of Eggenfelden. We hope that we will spend the night there, but we march on to the village of Bad Griesbach, where we find a barn. We wait in vain for some bread. Hungry and tired we cram ourselves in the straw. There is nothing to eat again in the morning. We depart for a nearby hill on which there are three farmhouses. We camp there, and at least we are not going further. They don't know what to do with us, but we are grateful that at least we can rest our legs. At noon we finally get three little potatoes, and in the evening our first bread, half-baked from barley flour. Never in my life has bread tasted so good.

We remain in that barn until Tuesday morning. Some of the prisoners who were sick in the camp and had remained there catch up with us here. Among them is Dr. Szamek from Bratislava. In the camp, where I was sedentary, the hunger bothered me more. At least on the march the changing scenery brings new impressions to mind, in spite of the gunfire in the back of us. We are sleeping on top of manure, and black flies that bite ferociously now join the lice. It is impossible to sleep.

It rains incessantly for two days. The field in front of the barn is a lake of mud. As we survey the terrain we think of a way to escape. Kapo Hans told us on Sunday, April 29, that Bavaria has surrendered, which would mean technically that we are now free. Many prisoners embrace each other in joy, but I am more reserved as long as we are under the bayonets of the SS. Being careful, I try not to show my emotions, but at night we welcome the sound of the distant guns. However, we already heard them in Plattling and still we are in the SS's grip. During the night from Monday to Tuesday, the rest of the kapos desert, as well as some prisoners who assist them, and some SS guards also.

Our old commander is still with us. On Tuesday morning [May 1] our cook is able to get a piece of a horse in Eggenfelden, but there is no time to cook it since we begin to march again at 9:30 a.m. Some prisoners cut off pieces from the horse, and one even takes a whole foot with the horseshoe intact. Perhaps there will be a chance to cook the meat somewhere.

It is raining as we leave the safety of the barn. Our legs are rested so perhaps we will be able to go on. Tonda has had a bad toothache for three days now, and Egon Horpaczký has a swollen leg and is worried about the march. Tonda's boot is also coming apart in the back. He stuffed a towel there to prevent the sand from entering, but it does little good. Before we leave we get a half-baked piece of bread. And so we continue the journey into the unknown.

On the way it is rumored that we are headed for the concentration camp at Mühldorf, but it is 36 kilometers away. We could reach it by nightfall. We cross a bridge that has been mined before the town of Altötting. It is situated on a hill and houses a field hospital. After passing through the neighboring town of Neu-Etting in the rain, we have the impression that the paved road we are on leads to Munich. We continue to hear loud explosions of gunfire, but it seems too near to be the Americans, so perhaps it is from some practice field. As we drag ourselves along the road we pass a heap of half-rotten beets. The prisoners hurl themselves at it despite the blows of the gun butts. The hunger is cruel.

Only about 4 kilometers from Mühldorf we turn to the left, in almost the opposite direction, and head for a patch of woods where we can rest. Those who have some of the raw horsemeat now eat it. As Tonda is chewing his, he throws a piece of skin away, and a hungry Pole pounces on it. That's what it has come to. We resume our march on rain drenched field paths. After such a short break our legs hurt again until we get them going. It is becoming dark, and Tonda says that he can't go any further. We tell him he must endure it, and in the end I tell him to hang on to me. And so we continue for another 18 kilometers. I don't know where I got the strength that I could drag Tonda along for all that miserable way. At last, in the dark as the snow becomes mixed with rain, we stop at another barn, utterly exhausted. There are fights over space. I myself fight with some German Jew. But Honza and I find a trough for oats, and together we go to sleep.

In the morning we all fill our cups with the oats and chew them as we march on. But we get a nasty surprise as we look out, since everything is covered with snow. When it melts we will all swim in mud. We get three small, half-spoiled potatoes. I eat them but am full of doubts whether it is wise.

The going through the mud is terrible. In a village we learn that the Führer has bravely given his life in the defense of Berlin. I hope it is true.

We come to a wood, and as we approach a grove of spruce trees several prisoners vanish. The SS open fire. As we continue through the woods, Honza and I try to estimate how far we are from our guards. We are without our commander, who left us yesterday in Neu-Etting. Our leader is now a man named Kowalski, a Pole, who is more considerate than the commander. I never saw him deal harshly with prisoners, not even swear at them. At times he has to shout, but on the whole, considering these times, he is a decent man. In Plattling I often did work for him, and now I try to stay close to him. I have such confidence in him that perhaps if I could not go on, he would not permit me to be killed.

The prospect of escape is very tempting, although it means being at least two days in the woods and hungry, before any traces of us will disappear or until the Americans find us. We are constantly evading them by changing our course. If only there were no snow on the ground, then at least one could find a dry place in the woods to sleep next to a fire, even though one is hungry. My boots are soaked for the second day running, and although I know I can stand it, at least we have had a roof over our heads at night. In two days in the woods in this weather, and in our rundown condition, one could easily catch pneumonia. These are the reasons why I cannot decide easily, even though Honza, who is eleven years younger than I, says quietly that at a sign he is going. As he says this, he jumps among the trees, as do several others, and disappears. Shots ring out after them. God go with you, friends! You have put your trust in escape, and at least, if you are killed, you will be killed as free men.

Before noon we are skirting a village where army supplies like boots, coats, and shirts are being distributed in a great hurry from a supply warehouse to the local population. This is a good sign that the end of Nazi rule is coming as the front approaches. We often hear the din of gunfire. In the next village some of our SS are going with the most trusted prisoners to "organize." This term in our situation means: what you cannot beg, then steal, and what you cannot steal, beg. The SS accompanies the prisoners to some home to beg for a piece of bread, since the prisoners cannot go alone. Then the prisoners divide what they get with the guards, as they are also hungry.

On one of these group "organizations," Tonda Bondy disappears. A friend of mine hypothesizes that Tonda is already dead. But within an hour Tonda is back, swearing. He had hidden in a building and was going to wait until it was safe to continue. But a German patrol found him, and when Tonda told the officer that he could not go on in his broken wooden shoes, he sent him back to the march anyway. What luck!

Nevertheless the thought of escape is constant. But I would like to have some bread, in case I have to spend two days in the woods hiding until the escorts of our march are 70 kilometers further. Then I can go begging myself. If a person is hungry with snow on the ground he is twice as cold. I feel that something must happen soon. I have had enough of this constant marching in mud. But I have to be sure because flight is a double gamble for one's life: if you escape the bullet, you may still perish from hunger or fever.

By noon on May 2 we wearily enter the town of Trostberg. We are mere shadows of our former selves. Even the men in town cry when they see us, and the dislike of the SS is now openly expressed. People are throwing bread from the windows, bringing potatoes or dessert, and one even came with a pot of goulash. We have to gobble it up quickly since we have to keep moving, but the SS are not preventing us from accepting food. I am now walking alongside an SS guard, a German from Slovakia, who suggests that I work my way to the back of the march and he will let me and another prisoner, Roubal, escape. He himself might join us. The SS man and I go up to a house, and a seventeen-year-old girl with an intelligent face immediately calls her mother. She gives us bread, potatoes, and a piece of meat loaf. That is my first and last effort at "organizing" as they called it, but really simply begging. We divide the food among the three of us and march on behind the others crossing a bridge.

On the way we discuss our escape. In any event, I do not want to march much longer. In the afternoon I would like to break away, now that I have had something to eat, and I have some bread saved. I am among some good people, and it might be possible to get food from some of them. Beyond the bridge we encamp among some bombed out German equipment. In the adjoining buildings we discover some Czechs who have been conscripted to work there. They happen to be on their break. Tonda had received some tobacco from them. They too think that the end must come at any moment, and some have even received their severance papers so that legally they are free.

I ask our guard where we are going next. He says he doesn't know yet, but the manager of the factory has prepared some food for us. It looks promising. We receive a portion of good soup and some bread. Now in any case I am prepared to withstand two days of hiding, and by that time the front will be that much closer. Then I will have to somehow cleverly cross over to the Americans and the death march will be over.

But our calculations are premature. After lunch we huddle again, but they have prepared a little train for us—a locomotive and two cars. There's a fine kettle of fish! I wanted to disappear in the afternoon and now I am off to parts unknown. In the cattle wagon I debate what to do next. We pass through some wooded hills and see many soldiers, armored vehicles, cars, and guns. Something is about to happen.

We disembark at Bad Empfing. As we march through the town there are field hospitals and army units everywhere. On a side street a woman with her daughter brings us in her bag some sliced bread and a few apples. But our prisoners, mostly those from Eastern Europe, almost trample them. They are so unruly that even the butts of the guns cannot restore order.

This scene arouses the animosity of the civilian population against the SS. One woman fearlessly makes some threatening remarks against them. Our condition elicits anguish and terror simultaneously among the civilians. That is how we appear. The command to resume marching is given to bring the situation under control.

We pass along several side streets, cross the river (Salice, perhaps?) and come to a distinctive Bavarian town, Traunstein. We are going to sleep in a pigsty on a bare cement floor, and there will not be room for all of us. "My" decent guard let me sleep in one of the feeding troughs that had some dry leaves. At least I did not have to sleep on the bare floor in my wet clothes and soaked boots. Originally, he had saved the spot for himself, but better quarters were found for the SS. There are eight of us there, pressed together like sardines, but at least we are warm. By morning new snow has fallen. At roll call there are only eighty-eight of us left. We get a little terrible soup but no bread. It is May 3—a memorable day in our lives. The boys in the pigsty find a container full of carrots so we have a "treat" for breakfast and some for the way. This is our last breakfast as prisoners. I am determined to disappear today, since I also found out that our commander had given the order not to shoot any fleeing prisoner. The guards can only shoot into the air, to prevent a mass exodus. I also observe that the SS are beginning to think more about themselves than about us.

Not long after the march begins we have to stop to let some army cars pass. That is repeated several times. Here and there we see civilians also fleeing with their belongings loaded into hand-pushed carts. For the most part they are well dressed and have evidently lived a good life. Probably, they are prominent Nazis who do not want to be captured by the Americans. Now they are trudging through the same muddy snow. We are having April weather: one minute there is snow and rain, and the next the sun is shining. On the left side of the road, artillery shells are stacked like a cord of wood. Obviously, this is in preparation for battle. God be with us if they begin to use them. Today we are supposed to reach Salzburg and from there further into the Tyrol Mountains. Salzburg is about 40 kilometers further, but I don't want to trudge that far in this weather. I want to disappear at the earliest opportunity. But the little settlements we are passing through are full of SS and soldiers, some of them Hungarian. Also, there are only a few farms.

Around ten o'clock there is a traffic jam of army vehicles that suddenly materialized among the mixture of retreating German soldiers. The cars are full of soldiers and SS, with officers in better vans, intermixed with armored vehicles, tanks, and even some horse-drawn vehicles. Most of the troops are Hungarian. Some vehicles are in the ditch—out of commission. We prisoners have ceased to be an organized march but go on in smaller groups interspersed among the troops, but still under the watchful eyes of our escorts. It isn't quite chaos yet, but a far cry from the usual German order. On the muddy road I see the trunk of our commander Kowalski that our prisoners have had on a pushcart all the way from Plattling. But those prisoners disappeared and the guards and SS then carried the trunk. Now it is lying forlornly in the road—further evidence that the last vestiges of discipline and respect for authority are vanishing.

Sometime before noon our SS guards huddle and, goaded by their superiors to be rid of us prisoners, tell us that those who cannot go any further are on their own. They in turn begin a fast march with which we cannot keep up. Now there are only fifty of us left and small groups begin to peel off. I am with Roubal and also with Sedlář, who had helped the partisans in the Slovak uprising in December 1944, for which he was arrested. He came with us to Flossenbürg and then to Plattling, and had a wound on his chest from a Kapo's blow with an iron bar. We drag on, accompanied by the SS, Jozko, and are all looking for the right moment when we can see some farm where there are no troops. It looks like we are still being guarded and that has its advantage, especially when we are standing by the side of the road weighing whether this is the right moment to begin our road to freedom. A military police officer from the Wehrmacht challenges us and asks us why we stopped. We tell him that we are on the road to Salzburg, but we are tired and need to rest. When Jozko confirms our story, the officer leaves.

Jozko then begins to march briskly on and we walk slowly for about two more kilometers to the village of Oberteisendorf. We leave the main road there. Roubal wants to turn right into the village, and I want to go left. It is funny because nothing makes any difference any longer. All we want is for this awful march, the hunger, and the lice to end. I see hills to the right, and that is another reason to leave the road, since I do not want to climb into the mountains.

We take a path through the field toward two farmhouses. Roubal goes to the second one a little further on, and Sedlář and I to the nearer one. Sedlář is in such bad shape that he cannot last more than a few days longer. He tells us later that he could not have marched another two days. None of us are much better off.

That field path from Oberteisendorf to Lohstampf is our road to freedom. We are planning to go through the woods and skirt the villages, heading back toward Traunstein to Trostberg. On the way we hope to meet the American army. But first we need food and rest. As we come to the first farm I see an older bearded and red-cheeked man, smoking a pipe, throwing out manure. I suspect he owns the farm, and from afar in a loud voice I greet him and ask if we can get anything to eat. He nods and we know we are going to get a bite. When I knock on the door an older farm-woman, who still has black hair and red cheeks, answers. I make our request, but she does not chitchat since we must look terrible in our striped prisoner garb, unwashed, and covered with mud. But in a short while she brings us some soup with a dumpling made of dark flour. Obviously it was left from lunch.

As we are eating I tell her who we are and where we are coming from. Her daughter-in-law joins us. Her husband is in the army. They listen intently, and the younger woman also brings us some potato salad. In the meantime a group of soldiers appear in dark uniforms with an eagle on their sleeves, presumably a part of the SS, also looking for food. But they get only some milk. Two of them come inside and one makes small talk, and as self-protection I talk with him. They are Germans from Slovenia in Yugoslavia who were working for the Todt Organization [a Third Reich civil and military engineering group in Germany named after Nazi leader Freid Todt]. Six days ago in Munich their weapons were taken from them and they were dressed in SS uniforms. They know that the war is lost and they long to get back to their families in Yugoslavia.

One of them shows me a map marked with the positions of the American and Russian armies in southern Bavaria and Austria. We seem to be in a confounded corner of the Third Reich where the last battle of the war may be waged. That could be a real fight in which we might still lose our lives. In case we cannot find any other shelter for the night I ask our hosts if we can stay in their barn or pigsty. We thank them for the lunch, say good-bye to the Germans, and go to find Roubal.

He too has had good luck and come to good people. They are poor but have big hearts. The farmer who had just hosted us owns that farm too, and the renter is a bricklayer, Georg Gillinger. He lives there with his wife and son, Sepp, who was exempted from military service because he is "feeble-minded" (retarded), which is quite common in the mountains. Their three other sons were all killed in the war. Inside the house we are welcomed in a friendly way by a German army deserter, Johann (Hans) Steinbacher. He is a barber from Hammerau near Bad Reichenhall and had already been sheltered there for a week, after a 120 kilometers march, mostly at night, through woods in which he hid. The Gillingers are very sympathetic and even though they themselves live only on their allotted rations, they immediately give us their last.

Hans produces a bottle of red wine and we have to drink to celebrate our freedom and to a better future.

He also gives me a shirt and underpants so that I can discard mine. That is the first step in getting rid of the lice. Now I simply have to catch and kill those left on my body. We are also able to wash and shave, and we feel like new men. Hans served in the Wehrmacht as a junior sanitation officer, so he knows what we most need. He also gives us cigarettes, and I have my first one in six months. In a little while, the brother of our hostess appears. He is also a deserter and with him are two Hungarian soldiers. It is about three o'clock in the afternoon, and the first American tanks can be seen on the road. A defensive line of artillery, manned by SS, is situated about ten steps behind our cottage, within range of the highway. Two women with their children now come to the house. They are Austrian refugees.

There are now about twelve people in the room when the first American shells explode about 200 meters from us. The cottage is shaking, and the women are crying and trembling with fear. Only the baby in the carriage is sleeping peacefully. We are comforting the women, as this is nothing new for us. We are used to such bombings since in Plattling we experienced frequent air raids.

The Germans are beginning their defense. Already nineteen of them have been killed. The rest of the disheveled SS are coming into the cottage to dry out and get warm. One uniformed nineteen-year-old declares that they will continue to resist. We are not feeling too safe since we are still dressed in our prisoner-striped rags and the red triangle next to our number indicates that we are political prisoners. That makes us his enemies. Here we are face to face in the last phase of this long and terrible conflict. We are here with a clear conscience in our fight for human freedom and dignity, but they consider us their enemies being locked into their senseless, fanatical Nazi ideology about being a superior race, which drove them into terrible collective and personal crimes inflicted on both nations and individuals. It is obvious that they are worn down by their long retreat and continuing battles. Even when they talk with great fanfare about victory, they no longer believe it. They are armed to the teeth and still carry out orders, but only an orderly retreat into the Tyrol Mountains makes sense to them. There, they hope to find shelter somewhere.

The thinking in the German army is interesting. All who retreat or run before the American army have only one destination in mind: the Tyrols. In their minds that is the only safe goal, as if the mighty American army with its superior equipment and support from the allies couldn't occupy this little area in a few days, even if it is very mountainous. Tyrol became the latest manifestation of their psychosis.

The grenades are exploding a little way off, and there is always a black cloud of smoke and dirt. We hear gunfire from rifles and machine guns. We are at the front. We hope it will all end well. The Germans will have to retreat since their artillery does not seem to be reaching the American guns, and they will not be able to withstand the onslaught from the allied guns, tanks, and planes that has now begun. I go outside the house so that I can observe a little, but I return quickly when I overhear the sharp order by the SS officer in charge above our cottage: "Shoot all bandits." Was he referring to us in our prisoner rags, or was it a command for his troops to fire on the Americans? To be safe, I told the others to sit where they could not be seen through the window.

About 40 meters away, a horse with his rider has fallen into a stream and is unable to gain his footing in the rain-soaked field. The rider tries to cajole the horse to stand, but after not having any success, a pistol shot rings out. The magnificent young animal tries once more to rise, but then lies down on his side and his fight is over.

Shortly after that as the evening approaches, an SS man comes into the cottage for his friend, who is warming himself. They are all leaving, apparently being ordered to retreat. The field is gradually vacated until only a few horses run freely. Hans and Sepp set out to capture them, and they succeed in catching two. Sepp elatedly declares that now he can be a farmer who owns a horse! It has cleared up, and near the other farmhouse where we were at noon we see a truck burning with its cargo of munitions exploding. The German resistance at Oberteisendorf is overcome.

As I go out, the sun comes out and is setting in the west. I am enchanted to see the Alps suddenly loom in the distance. On the road the rumbling of the American tanks toward Salzburg continues. In the distance I can hear artillery as the Germans probably are guarding the town. Later I find out that the Americans attacked Salzburg from the opposite direction from Freilassing and therefore the SS with whom we were marching and the other SS never reached it. The Americans got there first. I now have the definite feeling that we are no longer under German domination and we are free.

Freedom

At the same time I feel considerable hunger. We eat by the light of an oil lamp. Mrs. Gillinger, whom we call mother, cooked a potato soup, with potatoes in sour milk [considered a delicacy]. With us at the table are two Hungarian soldiers. I am almost ashamed how fast my potatoes disappear, as I have never eaten as much in my whole life. But I just survived starvation and a ten-day death march, so it is no wonder that I devour so much. Immediately after supper Sedlář lies down on the sofa. He is the most exhausted of all of us, and he still has the wound on his chest. He is soon asleep like a log. The other women left earlier with their children.

All of us men are now left in the room with Mrs. Gillinger. Her brother, Hans, and I recount our experiences. We are lucky that we have come to a village that remained opposed to the Nazis. Only the local schoolteacher had joined the Nazi party. Hans was also opposed to the party, as he is a good and friendly person. He invites us all to visit him in Hammerau after he returns. He is offering sincerely to help us as much as he can. He tells us how he had to defend himself so that he would not be inducted into the SS, and how, as a result, he was in constant danger. We drink black coffee from Hans's army rations and smoke cigarettes. All of us feel that we have survived a momentous era, and that this is the end of a terrible slavery to which millions of Germans and other people were subjected. At last we are free of Nazi terror that ended thanks to the American army.

There is a knock on the door. Who can it be at ten o'clock at night? Mr. Gillinger and Hans go into the hall to investigate. A voice can be heard as he steps out of the shadows. A man in his thirties in civilian clothes with a pack on his back enters. He is sturdy but appears weather-beaten in spite of the fact that he is wearing a raincoat, and he is obviously very tired. He is another army deserter. He started his journey six days ago from the mountains, and the last two nights he slept in the woods. He is from Hamburg and is intending to walk there. After he rests for a while he speaks in crisp sentences. He says that after such a terrible defeat he would like to leave Germany. For the last two years he has not believed that Germany could win the war. He knows that life will now be difficult for Germans, but it is bound to be better than being in the front lines. He has sized up his future quite realistically, without sentimentality and without optimism.

We are preparing for the night. Roubal and I are going into the barn to sleep in the hay, while the other men will sleep on the floor in the house. We lie down fully dressed with our boots on, even though they are cold and wet. We still can't allow ourselves more comfort in case the fighting comes back and then we might have to run quickly to the Americans. It would be difficult to get dressed and put one's boots on quickly in the dark barn. The moon is shining and the snow on the peaks of the Alps is bright. I am unable to fall asleep since I am cold, and because of the stirring events of the day, the proximity to the front, and my newfound freedom. Mostly I am thinking of my freedom and the fact that the war must end in a few days since so many soldiers are deserting the front.

The sensation of freedom is sinking in. I can still hear the artillery in the distance, the rumbling of American tanks on the road, punctuated by machine-gun fire. I am reminded of Tchaikovsky's 1812 overture, and how appropriate it is for May 1945. I remember the suffering I have endured since my arrest on October 13, 1944, how my brother and Mila came to visit me in prison in Bratislava, and the evening of October 29 when Mila watched as I mounted the metal steps of the Bratislava police prison to my cell, number 19. She clutched her coat and suspected that the next day I would be handed over to the Gestapo in Brno. I had hoped that I would remain in Bratislava for a few more days and so fell asleep that night in my cell. In the morning I learned otherwise as I was awakened. I wondered about how Slovaks survived when in April the news reported house-to-house fighting in Bratislava, and about my mother and other relatives who were still under German occupation in Bohemia. Toward morning I fell asleep briefly.

I doubt that this cottage in Lohnstamf ever hosted such a motley company. "God, I thank you that I am free, and that as a result of all I experienced during the last seven months, which was a great trial, I have emerged victorious and with a stronger faith than I had before." That is my great gain from these turbulent times in my life.

The morning of May 4, 1945, greets us with full sun, and I am in a happy frame of mind. After a good breakfast we discuss what we should do next. On the highway we see a steady stream of cars full of American soldiers, tanks, artillery, armored cars, large inflatable pontoons, huge cranes, and smaller cars darting in between very quickly. Overhead there are many noisy planes. German soldiers and SS men are coming down from the mountains both singly and in groups, but already unarmed.

We dare to approach the road only in the afternoon after we see the first group of German prisoners being marched toward Traunstein, led by German cars waving a white flag. We get our first close glance of American soldiers at the pub near the road, next to a gas station. They are young boys, dressed in khaki with helmets on their heads and armed only with a side arm. They are just fixing a flat tire on a bicycle. They recognize who we are in our striped prison uniforms, and as we approach they extend a friendly hand to us. Since there are also Canadians among them, I tell them in French that we are Czechs and thank them for freeing us. I have to dab my eyes since I am shedding tears for the first time. It is a moving occasion for me as I realize that here are people who grew up on the other side of the world and came to fight for the same freedom for which we fought here.

One of these young soldiers goes to his car and brings back a box of cigars. We each take one, but he offers another. We thank him, but he is proffering the box again and gestures that we should take the whole box. We gladly oblige. We ask him where the American headquarters are and he says in Aach Thale, about 5 kilometers away on the road to Salzburg. He indicates that he will lend us the car, if one of us can drive, but unfortunately none of us can. He still gives us some matches since they are not to be had in Germany. So we each light one of our wonderfully aromatic cigars until it smells like bread baking in a cottage, and we set out walking on the road toward Teisendorf, about 3 kilometers away. We want to go to the town hall to see if we can get a ration card.

We have to walk very slowly and at the edge of the road, and we need to stop frequently. The road is filled with a continuous and fast-moving procession of vehicles. The tanks make the road shake. We wave at the soldiers, who are dancing on top of their cars, and we shout "Nazdar" (hello) at them, but it is drowned out by all the traffic. The soldiers wave back to us, but some of them are tired and lying down on top of the tanks. Both the soldiers and we are covered with dust since the air is thick with it. One soldier sitting in a tank turret is drinking champagne and soon the empty bottles are ending up in the ditch. In one of the tanks a black Senegalese soldier has a wide toothy smile, as there is a French division attached to the third American army. From other tanks we are thrown cigarettes, chocolates, and cookies. Although they are all tired, they clearly are elated by their victory. The joy of these young people is infectious and soon sweeps us up in it. Nazi Germany cannot resist this mighty show of soldiers and weapons much longer. That is now obvious to us. By the side of the road there are German cars, discarded rifles, all kinds of weapons, and burned out tanks with the dead soldiers still in them.

An American officer stops us on the outskirts of Teisendorf. When he learns that we are Czechs he opens a small warehouse for us that had been for German and Hungarian troops and invites us to take what we need. We help ourselves to bread, crackers, soap, tobacco, and various other items that we need, such as needles and thread, razor blades, and so on. We are returning with two full sacks, already experienced "organizers." For three days and nights there is a constant stream of vehicles moving toward Salzburg. The cloud of dust raised by the traffic envelops the trees, and they appear gray. We are absorbed several times into this stream of humanity on the road and share its enthusiasm for victory and freedom. We return each time to Lohstampf, where mother Gillinger is amazed at what we are bringing.

On my birthday, June 5, I lie down on the grass behind the cottage, enjoy the warming sun and appreciate the breeze coming from the snow-capped Alps. Along the highway the rumble of the traffic continues, punctuated by the protective airplanes above. I no longer feel hunger pangs because we have been eating properly as a result of our begging. I am enjoying quiet times now, following the storm I have lived through in the past months with its deadly vortex. An ant is crawling on the blanket I am lying on. I take it gently and put it in the grass. And then I realize that I am human again, aware of the feelings of every related being, even this ant, as it proceeds to hunt for its food in the grass.

I should end here. Later I will work on this account and put it in a more acceptable literary form but keep the description of the whole picture. We lived for a while in a camp "Strupau" at Berchtesgaden. We were there with American soldiers, Russians, Poles, Latvians, Lithuanians, Dutch, Belgians, French, Luxembourgers, Italians, and Yugoslavians. I would also describe how we Czechoslovaks said goodbye to our American commander and his dear boys, who really looked after us with brotherly love. Then we went on to Salzburg, where we stayed about a week, Munich, Stuttgart, Nuremberg, Bamberg, where we again got stuck for a week, and finally we arrived in Pilsen and first tasted our freedom in our native land. On July 6, 1945, in the morning we arrived in Prague.

APPENDIX 2: AUSCHWITZ AND DEATH MARCH
SURVIVOR LISELOTT BÄCHER FRAENKL

L ISELOTT WAS MY cousin. For all of the Backer family living in America, Canada, South America, or South Africa she was our "favorite aunt." She consistently refused to speak about her Holocaust experiences until 1986, when she was in her eighties. My cousin Paul and I persuaded her to tell us her story, but she insisted "no tape recorder." Thus, this narrative is written in the third person; it is our reconstruction of the conversation we had with her.

Liselott was married to Pavel (Paul), the youngest of three brothers who had inherited a thriving factory that manufactured agricultural equipment in Roudnice, about an hour's drive northwest of Prague. They expanded the business to several parts of the world. The oldest brother, Jiri (George) emigrated to Rhodesia in 1939 where the firm already had a branch. Karel (Charles), the middle brother—my father's closest friend—went to Argentina. Pavel and Liselott remained in Roudnice to take care of the business there. This is why the Bächers are scattered in different countries.

Her account began with the year 1941 when the entire Jewish Roudnice community was ordered to the train station by the Nazis to be deported to Poland. Liselott and Paul were taken to the Jewish ghetto in Łódź. There they and their daughter shared a very small room with another family of three. Luckily, the other family shortly moved elsewhere.

Łódź was a ghetto for forced labor. Pavel was an engineer and was ordered to build a smelting machine in the space of a few days. He had the knowledge to do that, but he told the Nazis he needed certain materials. "You NEED?" they shouted. "We are ORDERING you to do it. Don't bother us until it is finished—and you better finish it fast!" Somehow he was able to produce the machine. In the meantime, Liselott was assigned to repair discarded military uniforms for prisoners. These uniforms had to be re-sown so that inmates could be identified easily. Liselott was very thorough in attaching colored appliqués to the uniforms, but a friend told her, "Don't be so conscientious! If anyone ever escapes they might need to rip those markings off easily and quickly."

Liselott and her family were in Łódź until 1944 when the war was winding down and the Soviet army was approaching. Prisoners in the ghetto were given the choice to go west, away from the front, or stay and face an uncertain future. The Jews had to guess what the outcome of either choice would be. If they stayed they could be executed by the Nazis to stop them from talking, or they could be liberated by the Soviets. Who could predict what the approaching army would do? Liselott and her husband chose to go west, while most of the prisoners remained.

They ended up in Auschwitz and knew immediately it was an extermination camp and danger lay ahead. They were separated as soon as they alighted from the train—men to one side, women to the other. That was the last time Liselott saw either Pavel or her daughter. Pavel died in Dachau later. The women went to the showers to be decontaminated because they were covered with crab-lice. On the way Liselott saw a friend lying on the ground, someone she recognized; but she was forbidden to go to her and offer help.

After a few months in the camp, Liselott was taken to Breslau by train and forced to begin the grueling death march. She was already very weak from her ordeals and the march was to be about 100 miles long to Cheb, in the most western part of Czechoslovakia. The women covered 10–15 kilometers a day, while the men had to march 40. Another person on the march was Hanka Gluck, a friend of the Bächers. Hanka knew that section of Czechoslovakia, and Liselott learned that she was plan-ning to escape. Liselott asked to come with her. Hanka replied, "You can come beside me, but I cannot be responsible—I cannot take care of you." Liselott decided that she could not escape in her weakened condi-tion, and anyway she did not have good shoes. Later, reflecting on her decision, Liselott acknowledged that Hanka was right and she held no grudge against her.

Recalling her bad shoes reminded Liselott how she came to obtain a better pair. On the march a Nazi soldier said to her, "Clean my boots. If you do a good job I might give you a pair." Liselott replied, "I need polish and a brush." He repeated the words that were said to Pavel, "You NEED?" So she polished his boots with grass and spit and the shoes did shine. The German handed her a pair of shoes before walking away.

The death march continued. The route came very close to her home town, Roudnice, but Liselott didn't have the strength to escape. With great effort she continued to march to Cheb. Liselott described the kinds of Germans who supervised them. They were largely ex-soldiers who had been wounded at the front. The Nazis had to find some kind of work for these men even if it was make-work. The former soldiers were forced to march as guards of the prisoners and they were very resentful. Liselott knew there were other marches like hers taking place, and she was puzzled at the reason. From the Nazi point of view she wondered, "Why not shoot us all?"

When the death march reached Cheb, the prisoners were loaded on a cattle train to Bergen-Belsen, a notorious concentration camp located between Hanover and Hamburg in northwest Germany, a long distance from Cheb. In these last days of the war Liselott was the closest to death that a person can be. Her niece, who was also interred in the same camp, discovered her aunt and found a way to smuggle potatoes to her that were unavailable to the prisoners.

Liselott confided that many times during those years when she was at her lowest ebb, help appeared from somewhere. Something pulled her up a rung from where she had been and helped her survive another day. Here it was receiving the nourishment of stolen potatoes.

Then came the end of the war and liberation by Allied troops. A Swedish deputy, Count Folke Bernadotte, appeared at Bergen-Belsen to actively help the remaining residents. Later he served in the United Nations. Bernadotte issued an invitation to all prisoners on behalf of Sweden to come to his country to be given the best possible medical care.

This was a dilemma for Liselott. On the one hand, she had been close to death and was still in dangerous ill-health, and Sweden offered the best chance for her recovery. On the other hand, she was waiting for her husband. In Bergen-Belsen, Liselott saw men dropping like flies from exhaustion following their death marches. She realized she did not have the strength to make the arduous journey to Prague to find out about Pavel. She decided to go to Sweden.

On the train to Sweden, Liselott was given a bed with sheets. "That was heaven," she recounted. She had not had a bed—especially not one with sheets—since her deportation in 1941.

Someone stopped by her bed and asked, "What would you like?" and without hesitation she replied, "A cigarette." On another occasion another person posed the same question and this time she said, "A toothbrush and a book." Two women passed her bed and she called after them, "Lotte, Kathe." They turned around bewildered and wondered who had called them. "I am Liselott" she announced. They looked at her as if a strange object had just fallen from the sky; they did not recognize her. Then Liselott realized how transformed she must be—almost a different person.

Liselott must have been one of the most serious cases on the train. The Swedes took these cases off the train immediately at the point of entry at Kalmar where there was a Red Cross hospital. She stayed for three months having a fever the entire time and weighing barely seventy pounds. At this low point help came again in the form of two Estonian women who had lived through the concentration camp but were now sufficiently recovered to aid others. Liselott slept most of the time. One time when she awoke she asked them, "Aren't they going to feed us today?" The women told her, "You slept through it again."

A representative from the Czech Consulate in Sweden came to question all Czech citizens. He wore a surgical mask for protection, and when he heard that Liselott was from Roudnice he became very excited. "You are a Bächer from Roudnice?" he queried. "I don't know you," Liselott responded, "take off your mask, please." He was the nephew of the manager of the Bächer factory and they knew each other. The official then asked her the same question he did of others, "Give me the names of three people whom you want me to notify about you." The first name she gave was her husband, Pavel, second, two cousins in Sweden, and finally Eva Peček, another cousin living in America, in Scarsdale, New York.

While the hospital in Kalmar treated her very well, it was not equipped to offer the treatment she needed. Liselott transferred to Stockholm. She was in the care of a physician there who treated not only her physical needs but also her psychological and spiritual ones. As she gained strength he asked her, "Do you want to go to the theater, or a concert, a movie, out to supper?" Then he would take her where she wanted to go. Liselott's total recovery took six months, during which she made arrangements to emigrate to America, settling in New York City with help from the Pečeks.

When Liselott concluded her story, often with tears in her eyes, Paul and I were tremendously moved by what we had just heard. The recounting had obviously been very emotional for Liselott and we sympathized with her pain—we understood why she had not shared her account with us before. In past conversations with us, Liselott had always spoken English, but during this interview she switched to Czech, obviously feeling more comfortable relating this story in our language. After she ended the interview, Paul and I thought she seemed relieved to have told her story at last, after saying no so many times.

The family celebrated Liselott's centennial birthday a year before she died in 2004 at age 101.

APPENDIX 3: LETTER FROM NICHOLAS WINTON'S MOTHER, BARBARA, TO MY MOTHER, 1940

◆

MOVEMENT FOR THE CARE OF CHILDREN FROM GERMANY, Ltd.

BRITISH INTER-AID COMMITTEE

Telephone : MUSeum 2900 Ext. 59 ..

Room 59
BLOOMSBURY HOUSE.
BLOOMSBURY STREET
LONDON. W.C.1.

PLEASE QUOTE BW/EW

C Z E C H   S E C T I O N

3rd July, 1940.

Mrs. A. Baecher,
Battle House,
Bromham,
nr.Chippenham, Wilts.

Dear Mrs. Baecher,

re your son Ivan, Ser.1174

I have just received your card, and am
writing by the same post to Mrs. Miller.

As you say you are losing your post, will
you kindly let me know how long your employers would
keep you, and whether there is any chance, even if they
do not keep you, of Ivan staying on. I am asking this
because I want to tell Mrs. Miller the exact date on
which I have to place Ivan somewhere else.

By the way, would you consent to send Ivan
with your employers' children to Canada? If you feel
like doing this, please ask your employers to be good
enough to let you know the agency through which they
will send their children and how much it will cost.

Yours truly,

BWinton

CZECH CHILDREN'S SECTION

ACKNOWLEDGMENTS

——————◆——————

I WISH TO thank several people whose assistance was invaluable for this book to see the light of day.

First of all, I cannot adequately express how grateful I am to have Paula Fisher as my beloved partner for over a decade. She contributed valuable input in the writing of this memoir and extended helpful suggestions, support, and encouragement to me throughout our mutual undertaking. I refer to her as my "personal editor," but Paula went beyond what that term implies. Having a love of history, Paula was immediately fascinated by the story of my escape from wartime Czechoslovakia; and we spent many hours, over months, working on the manuscript for my book. Most of all Paula became a sounding board for ideas and helped me tackle dilemmas that arose. I also thank her for renewing my enthusiasm for the project when it seemed to wane. Without Paula this memoir may not have been completed and certainly not so expeditiously.

I thank Joan Parker who became my literary agent and extended to Paula and me some of her impressive knowledge about books. Joan became a valuable adviser who made the process of publishing a book understandable. Our first contact was through a phone call she made to me regarding a presentation I gave at Moravian College about being on a Nicholas Winton Kindertransport train in 1939. Joan suggested I consider writing a memoir and seek to have it published—an idea I had only vaguely considered. She offered ideas and gave encouragement through the writing process and beyond. I am most grateful for all that Joan has done.

Other professionals played important roles that enabled my manuscript to become this book and I thank them all.

Julia Abramoff, senior editor of Skyhorse Publishing, read the manuscript and shepherded it along to completion. I thank Julia for her suggestions that strengthened the narrative and helped support the research. Other staffers at Skyhorse were also supportive.

James Brown skillfully restored old family photos to their pristine condition as shown in the book.

Bill Byers, a professional photographer and personal friend, contributed his talent for composition and detail in more recent photographs.

Dan Traut, my patient computer guru, made day-and-night calls to rescue me from many wicked technology glitches.

Members of the creative writing classes I took at the Adult Learning Program listened to and critiqued the vignettes I wrote that are now integrated into the book. They improved the final product.